OECD Development Pathways

Social Protection System Review of Cambodia

OECD DEVELOPMENT CENTRE

This work is published under the responsibility of the Secretary-General of the OECD. The opinions expressed and arguments employed herein do not necessarily reflect the official views of the member countries of the OECD or its Development Centre.

This document, as well as any data and map included herein, are without prejudice to the status of or sovereignty over any territory, to the delimitation of international frontiers and boundaries and to the name of any territory, city or area.

Please cite this publication as:
OECD (2017), *Social Protection System Review of Cambodia*, OECD Development Pathways, OECD Publishing, Paris.
http://dx.doi.org/10.1787/9789264282285-en

ISBN 978-92-64-28221-6 (print)
ISBN 978-92-64-28228-5 (PDF)
ISBN 978-92-64-28250-6 (ePub)

Series: OECD Development Pathways
ISSN 2308-734X (print)
ISSN 2308-7358 (online)

The statistical data for Israel are supplied by and under the responsibility of the relevant Israeli authorities. The use of such data by the OECD is without prejudice to the status of the Golan Heights, East Jerusalem and Israeli settlements in the West Bank under the terms of international law.

Photo credits: Cover design by the OECD Development Centre.

Corrigenda to OECD publications may be found on line at: *www.oecd.org/about/publishing/corrigenda.htm*.

Foreword

In 2016 Cambodia crossed the middle-income threshold, marking the transformation from a largely agrarian economy to the latest Asian Tiger. At the same time, Cambodia recorded one of the world's most impressive declines in poverty over the past decade.

Sustaining this pace of progress will prove a formidable challenge, especially given headwinds resulting from climate change, an ageing population and global shifts in manufacturing. To accelerate socio-economic development and reduce vulnerability, the Royal Government of Cambodia (RGC) has established a Social Protection Policy Framework (SPPF) in 2017, outlining an ambitious vision to expand coverage and increase coherence between social assistance, social insurance and labour market schemes.

The Social Protection System Review *is intended to contribute to the implementation of the SPPF. It provides analysis and recommendations to lay the foundations for a comprehensive and sustainable social protection system. This Review is the result of collaboration between the OECD and senior government officials, researchers and civil society representatives in Cambodia. The Review was supported by the European Union Social Protection Systems Programme, co-financed by the European Union, the OECD and the Government of Finland.*

The Review adds to the debate on the role of social protection as an engine for human development and inclusive growth in developing countries in three important ways. First, it constitutes an effort to assess Cambodia's social protection delivery from a holistic system perspective, including social assistance, social insurance and labour market programmes. Second, it provides new empirical evidence on the dynamics of poverty and the poverty impact of social protection and fiscal policy. Third, it proposes concrete recommendations to systematise social protection, reconcile social protection and fiscal policy, and accelerate progress towards the RGC's SPPF.

We hope this study will offer new and useful ideas on the ways to anchor the extension of social protection in Cambodia in a broader human development and inclusive growth agenda, and ultimately foster Cambodia's transition towards prosperity and well-being.

Mario Pezzini
Director of the Development Centre and Special Advisor to the Secretary-General on Development
OECD

H.E Sokharom Lao
Secretary General
Council for Agricultural and Rural Development
Royal Government of Cambodia

Acknowledgements

The Social Protection System Review for Cambodia was prepared by the Social Cohesion Unit of the OECD Development Centre as part of the European Union Social Protection Systems Programme.

The team was led by Alexandre Kolev, Head of the Social Cohesion Unit, under the guidance of Mario Pezzini, Director of the OECD Development Centre and Special Advisor to the OECD Secretary-General on Development. The report was drafted by Riku Elovainio, Alessandra Heinemann, Alexandre Kolev, Alexander Pick and Caroline Tassot, drawing on background papers prepared by the Economic Policy Research Institute. Justina La provided research assistance.

The report was reviewed by OECD colleagues Willem Adema, Karolina Kozlowska, Andrew Reilly, Prasiwi Ibrahim, and Jingjing Xia. It also benefited from valuable inputs and comments from Vathana Sann (Council for Agricultural and Rural Development), Fiona Ramsey (European Union Delegation, Cambodia), Betina Ramirez Lopez (ILO, Cambodia), Ole Doetinchem and Sabine Cerceau (GiZ Cambodia), and Jürgen Hohmann (European Commission).

The Review benefited considerably from comments received during a Policy Options Workshop held in Phnom Penh in June 2016. Participants included H.E Sun Kunthor, H.E Kim Sethany, H.E Oum Samol, H.E Sann Vathana, H.E Tin Sokkhuon, H.E Vong Sondab, H.E Laov Him, H.E Ly Savuth, H.E So Khonrithykun, Keo Ouly, Mon Chansarak, Dr. Sok Kanha, Sok Sreyleak, Mech Sochetra, Hem Makphal, Sopheak Vatey, Kong Chanthy, Suon Rasy, Hourn Darlin, Yam Vannfak, Ngeth Chonsereibandith, Betina Ramirez, Inna Sacci, By Sokunthea, Pheakdey Sambo, Tith Sakhan, Chin Narong, Suon Nguon, Mey Yoeun, Lisa Sherburne, Ly Lengmonykeo, Say Ung, Pok Kimchoeun, Ole Doetinchem, Chea Sokha, Phorn Yoeum, Kelin Hui, Ok Malika, Marisa Foraci, Sovannarith Hang, Manny Sreysour, Pheng Sokrathna, Maki Kato, Song Chhiay, Kimsong Chea, Erica Mattehem, Uy Uyma, Chan Theary, Ben Scholz, Mok Vichetsackda, Sok Chheang, and Chhom Sokkea.

The OECD Development Centre's publication team, led by Delphine Grandrieux, turned the draft into a publication. The cover was designed by Aida Buendía.

The European Union Social Protection Systems Programme is co-financed by the European Union, the OECD and the Government of Finland.

This publication has been produced with the assistance of the European Union and Finland. The contents of this publication are the sole responsibility of the OECD and can in no way be taken to reflect the views of the European Union or the Government of Finland.

Table of contents

Tables

Figures

Abbreviations and acronyms

ADB	Asian Development Bank
AFD	Agence française de développement, France
ASEAN	Association of Southeast Asian Nations
BFC	Better Factories Cambodia
CARD	Council of Agricultural and Rural Development, Cambodia
CBHI	Community-based health insurance, Cambodia
CCCA	Cambodia Climate Change Alliance
CCCSP	Cambodia Climate Change Strategic Plan
CDHS	Cambodia Demographic and Health Survey
CDRI	Cambodia Development Resource Institute
CfW	Cash-for-work programme, Cambodia, World Food Programme
CSES	Cambodia Socio-Economic Survey
DfID	Department for International Development, United Kingdom
DHS	Demographic and Health Survey
EBA	Everything but Arms, European Union
EFAP	Emergency Food Assistance Project
EII	Employment Injury Insurance
EU	European Union
FfW	Food-for-Work programme, Cambodia
FRS	Cambodia Food Reserve System
GDP	Gross domestic product
GIZ	Deutsche Gesellschaft für Internationale Zusammenarbeit, Germany
GRET	Groupe de recherches et d'échanges technologiques, French NGO
HDI	Human Development Index, UNDP
HEF	Health Equity Fund(s), Cambodia
HIP	Health Insurance Project
IDPoor	Identification of Poor Households Programme, Cambodia
IFPRI	International Food Policy Research Institute
ILO	International Labour Organization

KHR	Cambodian riel
LCA	Latent Class Analysis
MoE	Ministry of Environment, Cambodia
MoEF	Ministry of Economy and Finance, Cambodia
MoEYS	Ministry of Education, Youth and Sport, Cambodia
MoH	Ministry of Health, Cambodia
MoLVT	Ministry of Labour and Vocational Training, Cambodia
MoP	Ministry of Planning, Cambodia
MoSVY	Ministry of Social Affairs, Veterans and Youth Rehabilitation, Cambodia
MoWA	Ministry of Women's Affairs, Cambodia
MPI	Multidimensional Poverty Index
NCDD-S	Secretariat of the National Committee for Democratic Development, Cambodia
NCDM	National Committee for Disaster Management, Cambodia
NEP	National Employment Policy, Cambodia
NFV	National Fund for Veterans, Cambodia
NGO	Non-governmental organisation
NIS	National Institute of Statistics, Cambodia
NSDP	National Strategic Development Plan, Cambodia
NSFSN	National Strategy for Food Security and Nutrition, Cambodia
NSPS	National Social Protection Strategy for the Poor and Vulnerable, Cambodia
NSSF	National Social Security Fund, Cambodia
NSSF-C	National Social Security Fund for Civil Servants, Cambodia
NYDP	National Youth Development Policy, Cambodia
OD	Operating District
ODA	Official development assistance
OECD	Organisation for Economic Co-operation and Development
OPHI	Oxford Poverty and Human Development Initiative
Prakas	A proclamation signed by a minister or inter-ministerial entity
PPP	Purchasing Power Parity
PWP	Public works programme
RGC	Royal Government of Cambodia
SDG	Service delivery grant
SEA	Southeast Asia
SEDP	Socio-Economic Development Plan, Cambodia

SHI	Social health insurance
SKY	Sokapheap Krousat Yeugn (health care micro-insurance scheme)
SPI	Social Protection Index, Asian Development Bank
SPPF	Social Protection Policy Framework, Cambodia
SSDM	Social Service Delivery Mechanism, NSPS, Cambodia
TVET	Technical vocational education and training
UHC	Universal health coverage
UN	United Nations
UN DESA	United Nations Department of Economic and Social Affairs
UNDP	United Nations Development Programme
UNESCO	United Nations Educational, Scientific and Cultural Organization
UNICEF	United Nations Children's Fund
UNU-WIDER	United Nations University-World Institute for Development Economics Research
USAID	United States Agency for International Development
USD	United States dollar
VAT	Value-added tax
VRG	Village Representative Group, IDPoor Programme, Cambodia
WFP	World Food Programme
WHO	World Health Organization

Executive summary

Cambodia today is synonymous with progress. A prolonged period of political and social stability since the Paris Peace Accords of 1991 has provided the basis for rapid economic development. Since the early 2000s, Cambodia's average economic growth rate has been among the highest in the world; the success of its garment industry, its attractiveness to tourists and the growth in construction have driven a transformation of the economy. Poverty has fallen dramatically as a result, accompanied by a decline in inequality. In 2016, Cambodia graduated to become a lower middle-income economy.

Yet Cambodia's gains are fragile. A significant portion of the economy has not yet escaped from extreme poverty, while many of those who have are just above the poverty line. Both groups are highly vulnerable to shocks. Broader measures of deprivation have fallen much less quickly than income poverty. Malnutrition remains a particular concern, especially among children. Moreover, Cambodia's long-term prospects are uncertain: its demographics will become much less favourable and climate change threatens to have a major effect. The economy needs to diversify if current growth rates are to continue and productivity levels are among the lowest in the region.

The Royal Government of Cambodia (RGC) has recognised the critical role that social protection can play in reducing poverty, improving living standards and providing a better future for the country. In 2017, the RGC published the Social Protection Policy Framework (SPPF), an ambitious vision for a social protection system in which a comprehensive set of policies and institutions operate in sync with each other and respond to the broader needs of society – both today and in the future.

Cambodia's current social protection system is at an early stage of development. The largest social protection intervention in terms of coverage is the Health Equity Funds (HEF), which provide access to healthcare and other benefits to at least 2 million poor and vulnerable individuals nationwide. By expanding the package of benefits offered by HEF, increasing their coverage of the informal sector and improving co-ordination between the HEF and social health insurance, Cambodia can make rapid progress towards universal health coverage.

Scholarships and school meals comprise the bulk of non-health related social assistance spending but their impact on poverty is small: not only is coverage very low but the level of benefits is also small. These programmes are concentrated in rural areas, they rely extensively on donor support and they have not been rigorously evaluated. They need to scale up to reduce poverty and improve human development indicators, and they would be more effective if complemented by social assistance for new-born children.

Technical vocational education and training schemes for informal-sector workers are the RGC's principal labour-market programme, though coverage is very low given the size of the informal sector. Donor-funded public works programmes have a long history in Cambodia but are highly fragmented; an opportunity exists to align these more closely to other social protection programmes as well as infrastructure or climate-change adaptation initiatives.

Due to high levels of informality, only a small proportion of the Cambodian population is covered by social insurance, leaving them extremely vulnerable to lifecycle shocks and economic downturns. Even individuals who are formally employed only have access to a limited set of social insurance arrangements. Workers in the formal private sector have access to employment injury insurance and social health insurance but not to a statutory pension arrangement. Public-sector workers, on the other hand, are entitled to pension, disability and survivor benefits but the provision of health insurance to this group is at a very early stage. Unemployment insurance does not exist for either group.

The current pension arrangements for civil servants and the military are not financially sustainable. These schemes run on a non-contributory basis, meaning they are financed through general taxes. They already absorb a large proportion of the social protection budget and their expenditure is rising fast. Enforcing contributions by public servants is essential to safeguarding spending on other social protection programmes.

A rapid expansion of social insurance coverage is required to protect the gains in poverty reduction and prepare for the ageing of the population. Integrating pension arrangements and other contributory arrangements across the public and private sectors will ensure equitable coverage for the workforce as a whole. The National Social Security Fund (NSSF) is developing the capacity to oversee the social insurance system. Quick gains in terms of promoting comprehensive coverage could be achieved by enrolling garment workers.

Administrative systems for social protection need to be scaled up at the same pace. The Identification of Poor Households Programme (IDPoor) targeting system should be applied across the entire country and run more frequently. Monitoring and evaluation systems should be incorporated in the design and implementation of social assistance programmes and the Cambodia Socio-Economic Survey (CSES) should serve as a resource for assessing the impact and coverage of social protection provision.

Developing these instruments within a coherent framework, as envisaged by the SPPF, is essential to their efficient operation and to ensuring the entire population is covered by some form of social protection. The SPPF should be complemented by a financing strategy to ensure that the new system is sustainable. This strategy should reflect the fact that revenues to the RGC are growing strongly, though social protection currently receives only a small proportion of public expenditure. The low coverage of social protection among poor households and the low level of benefits among those who are covered means that the fiscal system can leave these households worse off once the burden of taxation is taken into account.

The Social Protection System Review for Cambodia seeks to support the implementation of the SPPF through innovative, in-depth analysis and practicable policy proposals. The recommendations presented here reflect extensive collaboration with the RGC, both through interviews with key stakeholders from the social protection sector and through a policy workshop in Phnom Penh in June 2016, which brought together representatives of the RGC, social protection experts from civil society and key development partners.

Assessment and recommendations

Cambodia's social protection needs are evolving

Since 2000, Cambodia has posted one of the strongest and most sustained periods of economic growth in the world. Between 2000 and 2015, annual growth in its gross domestic product (GDP) averaged 7.8%, raising GDP per capita to USD 1 225 and reducing poverty rates from over 60% to 13.5%. The national poverty gap, which indicates the severity of poverty, fell from 21.8% in 2004 to 2.2% in 2014.

The sharpest reduction in poverty occurred between 2007 and 2009 and took place predominantly in rural areas, driven by increases in crop prices and agricultural wages. In urban areas, the sharpest decline in poverty occurred between 2004 and 2007 and was associated with a significant increase in the proportion of the workforce in salaried employment.

Inequality has declined sharply since 2009 and is the lowest in Southeast Asia. The Gini co-efficient fell by 22% between the 2004 and 2014, from 0.38 to 0.30. However, this overall fall in inequality hides a trend towards increasing inequality up to 2009 followed by a strong decline thereafter. Between 2004 and 2009, consumption growth was highest for households in the middle of the distribution; between 2009 and 2014, it was highest for households in the lowest deciles.

A large proportion of non-poor households are at risk of falling back into poverty. Imposing a vulnerability line at 1.5 times the level of the national poverty line shows that 55% of households were either poor or vulnerable in 2014. As a consequence, a relatively small income shock could dramatically raise the poverty rate.

Data from the Royal Government of Cambodia's (RGC) Identification of Poor Households Programme (commonly called IDPoor), a targeting mechanism administered by the Ministry of Planning (MoP), show significant movement in and out of poverty between 2011 and 2014. However, while transient poverty is dominant, chronic poverty persists. The determinants of poverty have changed since the early 2000s: it is no longer a predominantly rural phenomenon and working poverty is a growing problem. Household composition is a major determinant of poverty, with caregiving responsibilities, whether for children, people with disabilities or the elderly, as well as single-parenting representing a higher risk of poverty.

Despite progress in monetary poverty reduction, multi-dimensional indicators reveal significant deprivation. In 2014, the multi-dimensional poverty rate was 33%, more than twice the money-metric measure. In 2015, Cambodia ranked 143rd in the United Nations Development Programme (UNDP) Human Development Index (HDI), with a score of 0.555, the lowest in Southeast Asia after Myanmar. While most measures of deprivation have fallen, nutritional deprivation increased between 2005 and 2010 and remained above the 2005 level in 2014. While the regions affected by income and multi-dimensional poverty differ, non-income poverty is concentrated in rural Cambodia.

Maternal and child mortality remain high. In particular, the number of maternal deaths per thousand live births in Cambodia exceeds the rate in other countries in the region despite an almost threefold decline between 2000 and 2014. The chief causes of infant deaths in Cambodia are communicable diseases, maternal and neonatal diseases followed by water-borne and infectious diseases. Access to clean water and proper sanitation, preventive measures and adequate awareness would significantly reduce this toll.

Sustaining school attendance to the end of secondary school is a major challenge. Net enrolment in primary school (children aged 6-11) rose from 77% in 2004 to 85% in 2014. Enrolment was 40% for lower secondary, 20% for upper secondary and 12% for tertiary in 2014. Only 40% of those enrolled in lower secondary and only 20% in upper secondary were expected to complete the respective cycle in 2014/15.

At the same time, child employment rates are declining but remain high: 30% of individuals under 18 not in school cited the need to contribute to household income. Youth employment is high by international standards. In 2013, 74.5% of males and 68.1% of females aged 15-24 were employed.

Among the workforce as a whole, the level of labour force participation is among the highest in the world while the unemployment rate was below 3% in 2015. However, informal and vulnerable employment remains the norm. Cambodia also has one of the highest levels of working poverty in the world and the proportion of the labour force working excessive hours exceeds 40%. Pay and working conditions are especially poor for women.

Labour force participation is also high among the elderly. Poverty among this group is lower than for the population as a whole but the current reliance on informal assistance networks to support the elderly will be increasingly problematic as the population ages. Living with a disability in Cambodia is associated with increased risk of poverty and destitution.

Looking ahead, high rates of economic growth and continued structural transformation are forecast over the medium term. However, there are risks on the horizon: Cambodia's recent growth has been driven in part by the garment sector, which is highly vulnerable to a loss in global competitiveness, a downturn in key markets or automation. Diversification is necessary but won't be easy; across the economy, productivity levels are low relative to the rest of the region. Meanwhile, the agricultural sector is unlikely to sustain its recent robust performance but will nevertheless remain a critical source of livelihoods for many households. Rural areas' vulnerability to climate change, in particular rising temperatures, is a major source of concern.

Cambodia has a clear window of opportunity both for advancing its economy and for establishing a social protection system. Rapid economic growth has coincided with a declining dependency ratio – the number of young and old individuals as a proportion of the working-age population – as a large young population has reached working age. However, the population will age fast in the future and the dependency ratio will increase rapidly from the mid-2040s onwards. Moreover, the size of the labour force and population dynamics as a whole will be affected by international migration.

An emerging social protection system

The RGC has finalised the Social Protection Policy Framework (SPPF), which lays the foundation for an integrated social protection system. The SPPF sets out an ambitious agenda for reforming and scaling up social protection and is intended to realise the right to social protection enshrined in Cambodia's Constitution. The SPPF is aligned with the country's Third Rectangular Strategy, the socio-economic policy agenda for the Fifth Legislature (2013-2018).

Social assistance coverage is extremely low and the sector is highly fragmented. It also has a clear rural focus, meaning that the rapidly-growing urban population is largely excluded. Social assistance has two principal objectives: human development and emergency response. In the first case, the largest programmes are school scholarships (currently limited to certain grades) and school feeding programmes; both are intended to improve school attendance. There is a lack of interventions earlier in the life cycle that might improve health outcomes among mothers and infants and thus enhance the outcomes of the scholarship programmes. In terms of emergency response, the RGC has established a new programme to support parts of the population vulnerable to climate change and also makes emergency relief funds available on an ad hoc basis. However, it also continues to rely heavily on external humanitarian aid.

Cash for Work (CfW) and Food for Work (FfW) programmes have operated in Cambodia for close to two decades. However, labour market policies have gradually shifted from public works programmes towards initiatives designed to improve workers' skills. Technical vocational education and training (TVET) is the most important labour market programme, providing skills training to individuals of working age (18-59) in informal employment who dropped out of secondary school.

In general, social protection provision for vulnerable groups is very limited. Public care facilities for the most vulnerable children are being scaled back. The RGC does not provide direct financial support for the elderly. Plans to roll out an allowance for people with disabilities exist but are experiencing major implementation challenges.

On the other hand, there has been impressive progress in terms of health provision, particularly among the poor. Basic health coverage is at the forefront of social protection and universal health coverage (UHC) is an explicit goal of the SPPF. In order to achieve UHC, the RGC intends to consolidate and expand the Health Equity Funds (HEF) and social health insurance (SHI), which is being rolled out for formal private-sector workers.

HEF is a nationwide programme that has significantly improved access to health care services for poor and vulnerable households and has lowered out-of-pocket expenditures. However, even for those covered by HEF, non-financial barriers to accessing healthcare remain at play, meaning that those who have access to free or subsidised care often choose to visit private facilities instead.

Social insurance arrangements are poorly developed for formal-sector employees and non-existent for the informal sector, which accounts for the majority of the workforce. A statutory pension arrangement does not exist for private sector employees, though these workers are entitled to healthcare and income benefits in the event of employment injuries. Since 2016, a growing proportion of private-sector workers, especially in the garment industry, are covered by SHI.

Meanwhile, the public sector does not yet have access to statutory health insurance, though a decree for such an arrangement was signed in 2017 and awaits implementation. However, these workers have access to pension arrangements: the National Social Security Fund for Civil Servants (NSSF-C) and the National Fund for Veterans (NFV). Both these arrangements are run on a non-contributory basis, which raises major issues about their sustainability. Replacement rates for retired civil servants are adequate but pensions are low in absolute terms.

Statutory unemployment insurance does not exist for any part of the labour force. However, workers who have been with an employer for six months or more and are dismissed for any reason other than gross misconduct are entitled to severance pay. Female employees are entitled by law to 90 days of maternity leave.

Social protection and fiscal policy are currently not realising their pro-poor potential

The low coverage of social assistance means it currently has little impact on reducing poverty or inequality. Health spending, on the other hand, is pro-poor and coverage is growing. In rural areas, the percentage of persons living in a household with access to subsidised health care is 9.2%, compared with 4.9% in urban areas. The population reporting having access to free or subsidised health care is highest among the poorest consumption quintile.

Public spending on social protection is low by regional standards and it is not pro-poor. While spending on social protection increased between 2009 and 2015, transfers to the NSSF-C and NFV accounted for the majority of this expenditure and have absorbed any fiscal space that might have existed to expand or introduce other social protection programmes. Spending on retirement benefits by the NSSF-C and the NFV increased approximately sixfold and fourfold respectively between 2012 and 2016. These payments are received predominantly by wealthier households in urban areas.

A successful domestic resource mobilisation strategy and strong economic growth have significantly increased the RGC's spending power in recent years. This should facilitate the implementation of the SPPF in a gradual manner. Priority should be given to expanding social assistance and direct transfers. At present, the overall effect of fiscal policy is to increase poverty, even though the tax system is progressive. This is because existing social assistance benefits have little impact on inequality or consumption levels, while social insurance payments mostly reach the better-off. As a result, the social protection system is unable to offset the impact of paying taxes on poor households.

Key recommendations

Expand social assistance, placing an emphasis on human capital development

- Establish a comprehensive scheme for early childhood development, which includes health, nutrition, education and social care initiatives.
- Expand scholarships to cover more school grades and operate nationwide.
- Establish social assistance programmes in urban areas.
- Prioritise permanent social assistance programmes over emergency interventions in areas at high risk from droughts or other climate shocks.
- Promote public works programmes by linking them to infrastructure projects and schemes that improve resilience to climate change.
- Establish an appropriate mechanism to provide income support for people with disabilities.

Establish a long-term financing strategy for the SPPF

- Develop a costed action plan for the different measures proposed by the SPPF which takes into account likely timeframes and priorities, as well as different scenarios.
- Integrate the long-term financing strategy for social protection within the RGC's broader spending plans.
- Incorporate distributional analysis into the financing strategy to ensure that social protection and its financing sources do not worsen poverty overall.

Integrate pension arrangements for efficiency and equity

- Expedite the implementation of contributions by active civil servants to the NSSF-C.
- Explore the possibility of establishing a single statutory pension fund for the public and private sectors.
- Establish a single forum for planning pension arrangements for all population groups.
- Properly calculate the long-term financing requirements for the current NSSF-C and NFV and ensure this debt is explicit in the government's balance sheet.

Promote systematisation to achieve universal health coverage

- Expand and harmonise HEF to be a national system in preparation for its consolidation within a single operator.
- Develop the package of health services covered by HEF and consider extending its coverage to workers in the informal sector with a low capacity to pay into a contributory system.
- Leverage the consolidation of HEF, the extension of social health insurance and formalisation policies as ways of crowding-in informal sector workers.

Improve the information framework for an evidence-based social protection system

- Integrate monitoring and evaluation processes into the design of social assistance programmes and policies to ensure rigorous assessments of results and the identification of potential improvements.
- Increase the frequency and geographic coverage of the Identification of Poor Households Programme (IDPoor) targeting mechanism and promote on-demand registration, allowing it to gradually evolve into a single registry.
- Incorporate a social protection module within the Cambodia Socio-Economic Survey so that it can serve as a resource for assessing the impact and coverage of social protection.

Introduction

Heir to the ancient Khmer Empire, the Kingdom of Cambodia is a parliamentary constitutional monarchy located in Southeast Asia and bordering the Gulf of Thailand, between Thailand, Viet Nam, and Lao PDR. Its population of about 16 million is among the youngest in Southeast Asia, with half the population aged under 25. The population is predominantly Khmer. Other ethnic groups represent less than 10% of the population and are composed mostly of Vietnamese and Chinese. Cambodia is also among the poorest economies in Southeast Asia, with a gross domestic product (GDP) per capita of USD 1 225 in 2015.

The population of Cambodia has suffered substantially over the past decades from deep economic, social and political turmoil related to the rule of the Khmer Rouge in the 1970s, the Vietnamese occupation in 1978, and the ensuing civil war that lasted almost 13 years. Studies indicate that at least 1.5 million Cambodians died from execution, forced hardship or starvation under the Khmer Rouge regime.

The country has benefited greatly from the restoration of peace and stability achieved by the 1991 Paris Peace Accords. Since 2000, Cambodia's economy has posted one of the strongest and most sustained periods of growth in the world. The rapid expansion of the garment and footwear industry has driven economic development, increasing the role of the industrial sector and reducing agriculture's contribution to GDP and employment. This change in the structure of the economy has generated large-scale migration from rural to urban areas which, together with a rapid growth in the size of the working-age population, has transformed the labour market. This growth performance has been accompanied by a sharp drop in income poverty.

However, the challenge of securing livelihoods for all in the years to come remains enormous. Today, a large number of the population is near poor; informality and vulnerable employment are widespread, and human development indicators remain among the lowest in Southeast Asia. A range of social protection instruments aim to address these challenges but these operate on a relatively small scale and considerable gaps remain. Cambodia must also confront the profound threat proposed by climate change, harness the potential of rapid urbanisation and prepare for ageing of the population. There are additional concerns that without action to secure livelihoods, a number of emerging trends threaten to undo much of the gains achieved in recent years.

Cambodia's Rectangular Strategy for Growth, Employment, Equity and Efficiency places the goal of economic development and poverty reduction at the centre of national policy making. With this in mind, the Government of Cambodia has developed a Social Protection Policy Framework (SPPF) with a view to harmonising, concentrating and strengthening existing schemes in order to increase effectiveness, transparency and consistency of the entire social protection system. Meeting these objectives requires a close monitoring of social protection needs together with an assessment of the adequacy and equity of existing social protection initiatives. It also calls for a holistic approach that supports policy coherence across different public actions.

A principal objective of this report is to contribute to the ongoing policy dialogue on social protection, sustainable growth and poverty reduction. It prompts a series of questions that are crucial for the implementation of Cambodia's SPPF. How will emerging trends affect the needs for social protection, now and into the future? To what extent are Cambodia's social protection instruments able – or likely to address current and future livelihood challenges? How does fiscal policy affect social protection objectives?

This report is organised as follows: Chapter 1 is a forward-looking assessment of Cambodia's social protection needs. Chapter 2 maps the social protection sector and examines its adequacy. An investigation of the distributive impact of social protection and tax policy is undertaken in Chapter 3. The last chapter concludes with recommendations for policy strategies that could support the establishment of an inclusive social protection system in Cambodia, as envisaged by the SPPF.

Chapter 1

Forward-looking assessment of social protection needs in Cambodia

This chapter provides a forward-looking assessment of risk and vulnerability in Cambodia. While monetary poverty has fallen rapidly since the early 2000s and inequality has also declined, a large population is vulnerable to falling back into poverty. The analysis demonstrated that deprivation levels have not declined as quickly as monetary poverty. Climate change, large-scale internal and international migration, rapid urbanisation and changes to the age structure of the population are likely to determine demand for social protection over the longer term. The extent to which Cambodia is able to diversify its economy will also be a critical factor.

Since 2000, Cambodia has posted one of the strongest and most sustained periods of economic growth of any country in the world. The rapid growth of the garment and footwear industry has transformed the economy, increasing the industrial sector and reducing agriculture's contribution to gross domestic product (GDP) and employment. This has been accompanied by a sharp drop in income poverty and improvements in human development indicators. In July 2016, Cambodia officially graduated to lower-middle income status.

However, major challenges remain. Cambodia is still classified as one of the world's least developed countries, a large proportion of the population is near poverty, and informality and vulnerable employment are widespread. At the same time, Cambodia must confront the profound threat posed by climate change, harness the potential of rapid urbanisation, further diversify its economy and prepare for the ageing of the population.

This chapter summarises the findings of a forward-looking needs analysis that forms the basis of the Cambodia Social Protection System Review. Annex 1.A1 provides an outline of this tool, which is being applied for the first time in Cambodia. By analysing the socioeconomic context for social protection today and projecting how this context is likely to change in the future, this exercise is central to understanding how well the current social protection system responds to current needs of the population and how demand is likely to evolve.

Poverty has fallen rapidly but these gains are fragile

Cambodia has experienced dramatic increases in income and reductions in poverty. Between 2000 and 2015, annual growth in Cambodia's GDP averaged 7.8%, raising GDP per capita to USD 1 225 and reducing poverty rates from over 60% to 13.5% in 2014 (Figure 1.1).

Income poverty has declined at different times in rural and urban areas. The sharpest reduction in national poverty occurred between 2007 and 2009 and took place predominantly in rural areas, driven by increases in crop prices and agricultural wages. In urban areas, the sharpest decline in poverty occurred between 2004 and 2007.

The decrease in urban poverty was associated with a significant increase in the proportion of the workforce in salaried employment, which accounted for 50.5% of total employment in 2011, up from 36.6% in 2004 (World Bank, 2014a). The poverty level in Phnom Penh has fluctuated since the global financial crisis and, in 2012, exceeded the poverty rate in other urban areas for the first time (ADB, 2014).

Not only has the poverty rate declined but so too has the severity of poverty. The national poverty gap, which measures how far, on average, poor households are below the poverty line, fell from 21.8% in 2004 to 2.2% in 2014. According to data from the Cambodia Socio-Economic Survey (CSES)[1] for 2014, the poverty gap in rural areas was 2.2% and 2.6% in urban areas. This suggests that the majority of poor individuals are close to exiting poverty.

Box 1.1. **National and international poverty measures and terms used in this Review**

Monetary or income poverty: Poverty status based on either household consumption or income as household welfare metrics.

- **National poverty line (national; Royal Government of Cambodia (RGC)):** This poverty line is monetary and calculated using data from the Cambodia Socio-Economic Surveys (CSESs) for Phnom Penh, other urban areas and rural areas. It has three components: food expenditure; non-food expenditure; and spending on housing, energy and basic services. For 2014, the national monthly poverty line was equivalent to USD 46 per capita (current USD).
- **Vulnerability line (national):** The vulnerability line is equal to 1.5 times the national poverty line.
- **Food poverty line (national; RGC):** The food poverty line is the equivalent sum of money that is necessary in order to consume a minimum of 2 200 calories per person per day, averaged between those in the bottom 5th to 30th percentile groups of the population. The 2014 national monthly food poverty line in Cambodia was equivalent to USD 58 per capita (current USD).
- **Global poverty lines (international):** Poverty lines defined by the World Bank based on the 15 poorest countries in 2005. Until 2015, the poverty line was set at USD 1.25/day; in 2005 Purchasing Power Parity (PPP, computed on the basis of price data across the world), with an upper poverty line set at USD 2/day. Following an update of 2011 prices, the poverty line is now set at USD 1.90/day in 2011 PPP, with an upper poverty line set at USD 3.10/day.
- **Near poverty (RGC):** Households who are "near poor" are classified as non-poor but are located just above the poverty line, where shocks are likely to send them back under the poverty line. The term is not associated with a specific level of income or consumption.
- **Poverty rate (RGC):** The proportion of the population that lives below the national poverty line. For 2014, the national poverty rate was calculated at 13.5%, using the 2014 CSES.

Box 1.1. **National and international poverty measures and terms used in this Review** *(cont.)*

- **Poverty gap:** How far (on average) poor households are below the poverty line, expressed as a percentage of the level at which the poverty line is set.

Multi-dimensional or non-income poverty: Poverty status based on deprivations of a household in areas beyond monetary poverty.

- The Oxford Poverty and Human Development Initiative (OPHI) **Multidimensional Poverty Index (MPI)** covers three areas: education, health and standard of living through ten indicators: years of schooling, school attendance, child mortality, nutrition, electricity, sanitation, access to or cleanliness of water, conditions of the floor of their shelter, type of cooking fuel used, and assets. The indicators are weighted to create a deprivation score: a deprivation score of 33.3% indicates multi-dimensional poverty, a score of 50% or more indicates severe multi-dimensional poverty, and a score between 20-33.3% indicates near multi-dimensional poverty.
- The United Nations Development Programme (UNDP) **Human Development Index (HDI)** covers three areas: health, education and standard of living. It is a summary measure based on the geometric mean of normalised indices for each dimension (life expectancy at birth, average and expected years of schooling, gross national income per capita).

Cambodia Development Resource Institute (CDRI) wealth index: Poverty status computed in panel data through principal component analysis of five dimensions: agricultural land and livestock, demography, human capital, social capital and natural resources. Poverty lines are defined at the 40th and 60th percentile of the wealth index.

- **Transient poverty**: Households identified as poor but above the poverty line in at least one of four survey rounds.
- **Chronic poverty**: Households identified as poor and below the poverty line in each of four survey rounds.

IDPoor Programme poverty thresholds (national; RGC): The Identification of Poor Households Programme (IDPoor) classifies household income level using a proxy means test, which assigns a household "poverty score" based on a range of information, such as demographics, number of children in the house and indebtedness, to the cumulative quality and quantity of a household's assets.

- **Non-poor:** Households classified as "non-poor" have been assigned a PMT score that ranges from 0 to 44.
- **Poor ("IDPoor 1"):** Households classified as "poor" fall within a PMT score range of 45 to 58 points.
- **Very poor ("IDPoor 2"):** Households classified as "very poor" have been assigned a PMT score greater than 58.

Figure 1.1. **Poverty has fallen considerably over the last decade**

National poverty rates, RGC and World Bank (2004-14)

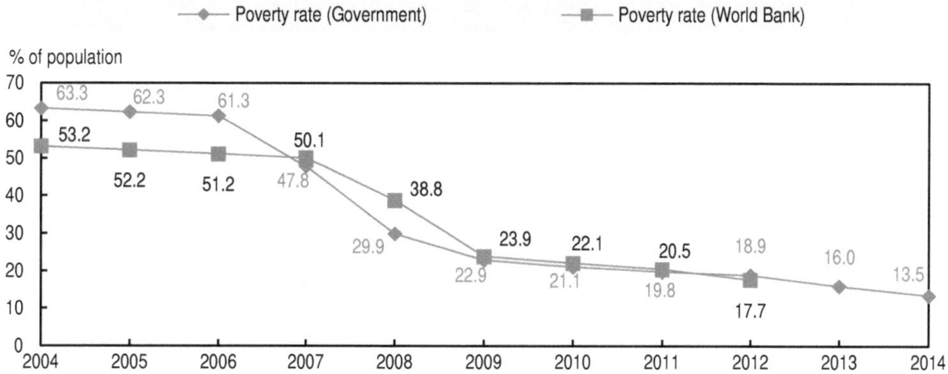

Source: World Bank (2014a), *Where Have All the Poor Gone? Cambodia Poverty Assessment 2013, documents.worldbank.org/curated/en/824341468017405577/pdf/ACS45450REVISE00English0260May02014.pdf.*

According to CSES data, the Gini coefficient[2] fell by 22% between the 2004 and 2014 surveys, from 0.380 to 0.295. Inequality has increased up to 2009 but declined rapidly thereafter (ADB, 2014). This is reflected in household consumption growth by decile between 2004-09 and between 2009-14 (Figure 1.2).

Figure 1.2. **Consumption growth has been pro-poor**

Consumption growth by decile (2004-09, 2009-14)

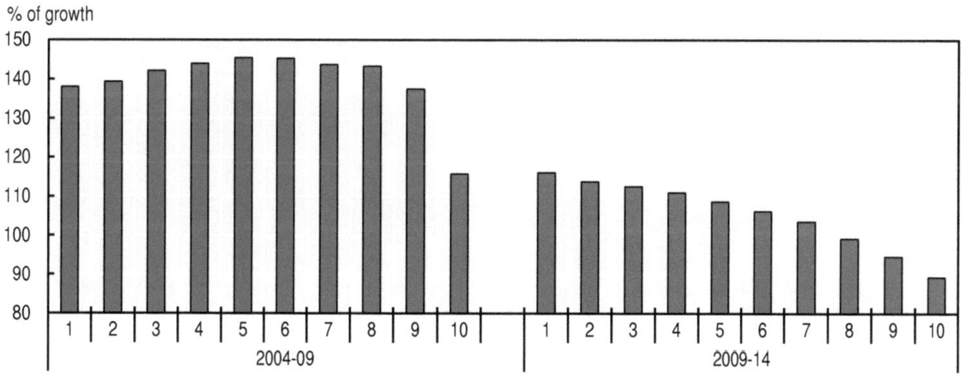

Note: *KHR = Cambodian riel

The deciles of household consumption in 2004 Cambodian riel (KHR) are defined according to the following cut-offs: 223 336 / 287 402 / 345 023 / 399 538 / 464 581 / 548 614 / 657 613 / 831 222 / 1 222 352. The deciles of household consumption in 2009 Cambodian riel (KHR) are defined according to the following cut-offs: 305 029 / 402 916 / 491 333 / 578 654 / 676 039 / 790 107 / 947 577 / 1 174 667 / 1 610 982. The deciles of household consumption in 2014 Cambodian riel (KHR) are defined according to the following cut-offs: 350 282 / 456 077 / 549 250 / 636 399 / 729 553 / 829 604 / 961 286 / 1 137 181 / 1 495 614.

Source: Authors' calculations based on National Institute of Statistics, Cambodia (NIS) (2004, 2009, 2014), *Cambodia Socio-Economic Surveys.*

Between 2004 and 2009, consumption growth was highest for households in the middle of the distribution. Between 2009 and 2014, it was highest for households in the lowest deciles. The decline identified for consumption among the top two deciles might reflect methodological difficulties in capturing consumption at the top end of the income distribution (ADB, 2014).

Cambodia has the lowest level of inequality in Southeast Asia. Inequality has fallen only slightly in the Philippines and Thailand, while it has risen in Viet Nam, Indonesia and Lao People's Democratic Republic (Lao PDR) since 2004.

However, this success is fragile. A large proportion of non-poor households (based on monetary poverty lines) are at risk of falling back into poverty. Figure 1.3 shows a clear shift in the distribution of household consumption across the population for 2004, 2009 and 2014. The majority of households move out of monetary poverty and a large number of poor households are clustered just below the poverty line.

However, many non-poor households remain just above the national poverty line. Imposing a "vulnerability line" at 1.5 times the level of the poverty line shows that 55% of households were either poor or vulnerable in 2014. This is lower than in 2004 and 2009 but very high nonetheless.

Figure 1.3. **While the poverty headcount has decreased, vulnerability remains high**

Cumulative distribution of household consumption in Cambodia (2004-14)

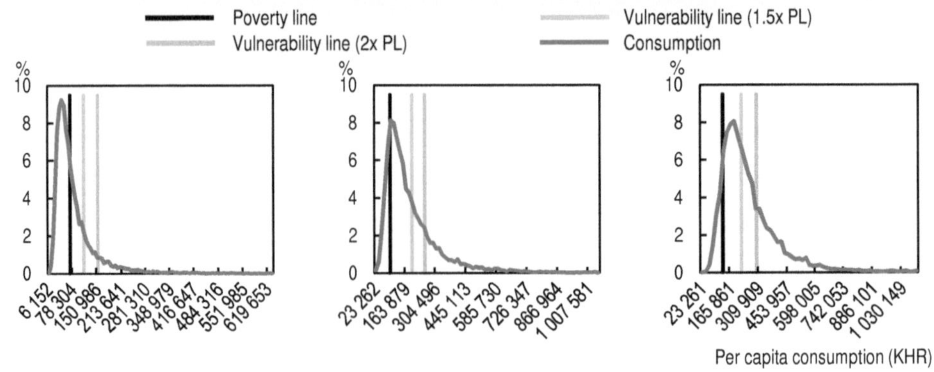

Note: KHR = Cambodian riel.

Source: Authors' calculations based on NIS (2004, 2009, 2014), *Cambodia Socio-Economic Surveys.*

The left-hand panel of Figure 1.4 shows how the headcount poverty rate would have increased in previous years if the national poverty line were adjusted upwards. The sensitivity is especially pronounced in 2014, due to the number of households that moved above the poverty line but remained below the vulnerability line. According to the 2014 CSES, an economic shock that reduced incomes uniformly by 20% would have nearly doubled the national poverty rate in that year. The right-hand panel of Figure 1.4 shows how poverty has declined according to international rather than local benchmarks. In 2014, Cambodia's national poverty rate would have been much higher if the new USD 1.90 benchmark for extreme poverty had been used instead of the national poverty line.

Figure 1.4. **Poverty rates are highly sensitive to small changes in the poverty line**

Headcount poverty rates in Cambodia, according to national and international poverty lines (2004-14)

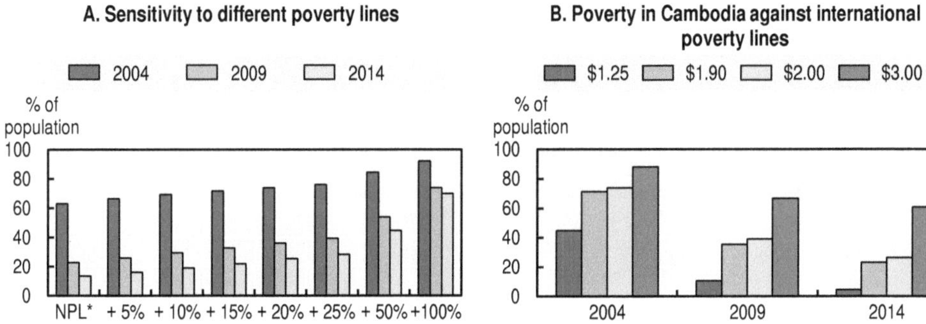

Note: * NPL = national poverty line (Cambodia).

Source: Authors' calculations based on NIS (2004, 2009 and 2014), *Cambodia Socio-Economic Surveys*.

The Identification of Poor Households Programme (commonly called the IDPoor system) is a registry of households that the RGC uses to determine eligibility for government or donor anti-poverty programmes. The database is administered by the Ministry of Planning (MoP) and follows households at intervals of about three years.

This report is the first to analyse the data contained within the IDPoor database, which provides valuable insights into the dynamics of poverty and vulnerability in Cambodia. Figure 1.5 shows transitions in household poverty over three IDPoor waves (time periods): 2008/09, 2010/11 and 2013/14.[3] Given that the IDPoor programme is principally applied in rural areas, this analysis mainly captures the dynamics of rural poverty from 2008 onwards, meaning that it covers the periods when rural poverty was declining rapidly and when this decline slowed.

Households categorised by IDPoor as poor or very poor show significant movement in and out of poverty. Over half of the households categorised as non-poor remained out of poverty over the three waves. Among those categorised as poor in each of the first two waves, about one-third transitioned out of poverty by the third survey, while one-third remained poor and one-third fell into extreme poverty. About half of the very poor in each of the first two waves transitioned out of poverty but about 6% fell back into extreme poverty thereafter.

These findings highlight the need for social protection mechanisms that protect the incomes of households who have emerged from poverty in the event of a shock that would otherwise send them back below the poverty line. Given the extensive clustering of households just above the poverty line, this shock would not need to be very big. Meanwhile, the existence of a cohort that remains very poor across the surveys indicates that Cambodia's economic growth is not benefiting all households equally and thus highlights the role for social assistance in achieving further gains in reducing poverty.

Figure 1.5. **Individuals frequently transition in and out of poverty**

Transitions in household poverty in Cambodia
(IDPoor waves: 2008/09, 2010/11 and 2013/14)

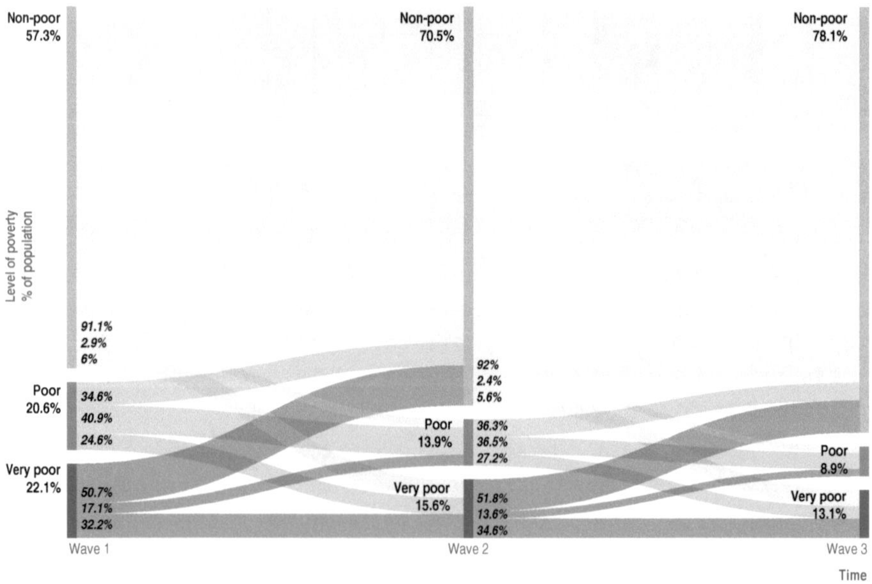

Note: This graph shows the movement of Cambodian households between states of welfare between 2008 and 2014. The population observed in this graph belong to a restricted subset of the IDPoor panel sample. The percentages listed in black indicate the share of households that fall under each poverty category within each wave. The percentages listed in black italics indicate the share of households within each category of poverty that make a transition to the next poverty state (indicated by the direction of the flow). The direction of each transition can be identified by the origin and end point of the flow. The nomenclature of the graph is that used by the IDPoor programme. Poverty categories are assigned according to the final scores of a proxy means test, described in Annex 2.A2.

Source: Authors' calculations based on MoP (2016), IDPoor data (2008-2014).

The poverty dynamics revealed by analysis of the IDPoor database are consistent with the findings of a four-round household panel survey conducted by the Cambodia Development Resource Institute (CDRI) between 2001 and 2011 (Tong, 2012). This study found that between 84% and 90% (depending on the poverty line applied) of households identified as poor across the surveys were above the poverty line for at least one of the four rounds, on which basis they are classified as "transient poor". Between 4% and 10% of sample households were below the poverty line in each of the four rounds, rendering them "chronically poor". By comparison, of the IDPoor households identified as very poor, more than one-third remained very poor across the three waves.

The composition of poverty has changed

The next step is to analyse the characteristics of the poor and non-poor households to understand which groups are most at-risk from remaining in poverty or falling into poverty. A technique called Latent Class Analysis (LCA) was applied to households identified as poor in the CSES for 2004, 2009 and 2014 to show how the characteristics of poverty have changed since 2004. LCA clusters sub-groups of poor households according to similarities in their socio-demographic profile and thus sheds light on the needs and characteristics of various groups within the poor population across the three surveys.

This exercise provides valuable insights for policy makers when considering the design and targeting of anti-poverty programmes. Figure 1.6 shows the results for each year, aggregating the poor households identified in the CSES for 2004 and 2014 into four groups, and those for 2009 into five groups. The size of the respective boxes in 2009 and 2014 reflects the size of each sub-group relative to the size of the poor population in 2004.

A large number of households characterised as poor across all three surveys are responsible for looking after children. The presence of persons with disabilities also placed households at higher risk of poverty across the three surveys, especially in 2014. The impoverishing effect of caregiving might reflect a reduction in household labour supply, a higher dependency ratio within a household (the proportion of those can participate in the economy relative to those who cannot), or both.

Possessing little or no education (defined as some members having completed primary education and no educated household members, respectively) is characteristic of the two largest clusters of poor households in each year, underlining the role education plays in improving livelihoods and the value of interventions aimed at keeping children in school. Without such interventions, it will be very difficult to help households escape from the poverty trap: poor households find it harder to send children to school or to provide them adequately with nutrition, with the result that these children are more likely to end up poor and the cycle thus continues.

Figure 1.6. **The profile of poor households is changing**

Latent class analysis (LCA) poverty clusters (2004-14)

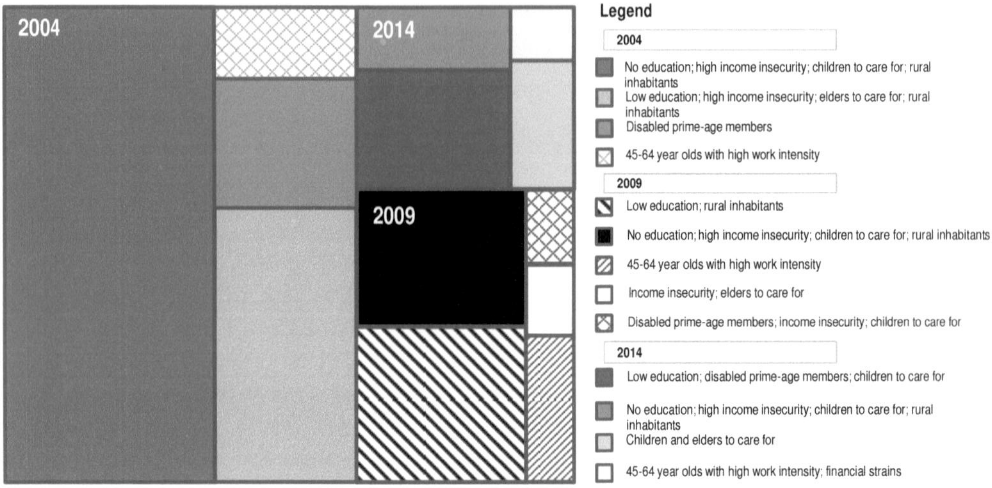

Source: Authors' calculations based on NIS (2004, 2009 and 2014), *Cambodia Socio-Economic Surveys*, available at *nada-nis.gov.kh/index.php/catalog/CSES*; and MoP (2016), IDPoor data (2008-2014).

As detailed in Chapter 2, the RGC and development partners are seeking to promote the development of children through scholarship and school feeding programmes aimed at improving school attendance. However, there are presently large gaps in these schemes, which do not operate nationwide and where they do operate, don't cover all the grades. There are no public transfers linked specifically to caregiving responsibilities; although financing has been made available for a benefit for people with disabilities, this has not been implemented.

While the two largest clusters in 2004 and 2009 consisted of people living in rural areas, rural poor are less prominent in the 2014 survey. This is consistent with the rapid decline in rural poverty between 2009 and 2014 and indicates that poverty is no longer just a rural phenomenon.

Although not identified specifically in Figure 1.6, the LCA shows that female-headed and single-parent households feature prominently among poor households, underscoring the impoverishing impact of caregiving responsibilities. Larger households are also at higher risk of income poverty. According to the 2014 CSES, only 3.5% of three-member households were poor, compared with 23.4% of those with seven members.

The LCA also reveals that many poor households have one or more wage-earners but employment fails to protect household members against poverty. Households reporting high levels of work intensity but exhibiting no other correlates of poverty (such as low education or financial burdens) feature across all three surveys. A minimum wage might improve this situation, though enforcement would be problematic given the high level of informality discussed later.

Deprivation has not fallen in line with monetary poverty

In 2015, Cambodia ranked 143rd in the United Nations Development Programme (UNDP) Human Development Index (HDI), with a score of 0.555, the lowest in SEA after Myanmar (Figure 1.7, which excludes Myanmar due to lack of historical data). In 2004/05, the national monetary poverty rate was 10% higher than multi-dimensional poverty; in 2014, the multi-dimensional poverty rate was 33%, more than twice the money-metric measure. In addition to the population classified as multi-dimensionally poor in 2014, a further 21.6% were considered vulnerable to poverty.

Figure 1.7. **Cambodia still lags behind its neighbours in terms of human development indicators**

HDI in SEA (1980-2014)

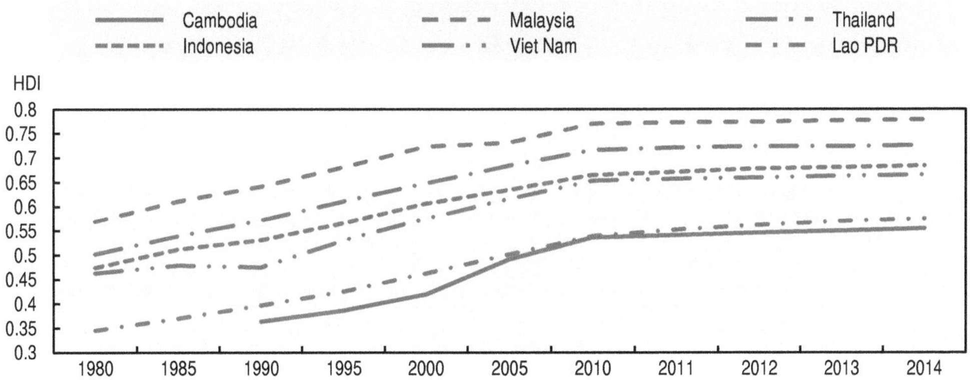

Source: UNDP (2016), *Shaping the Future: How Changing Demographics Can Power Human Development*, *hdr.undp.org/sites/default/files/rhdr2016-full-report-final-version1.pdf*.

Demographic and Health Survey (DHS) data for 2005-14 show regular and substantial declines in almost all deprivations except nutrition, which increased between 2005 and 2010 and remained above the 2005 level in 2014 (Figure 1.8).

Figure 1.8. **Most indicators of deprivation are improving**

Multi-dimensional poverty deprivations in Cambodia (2005-14)

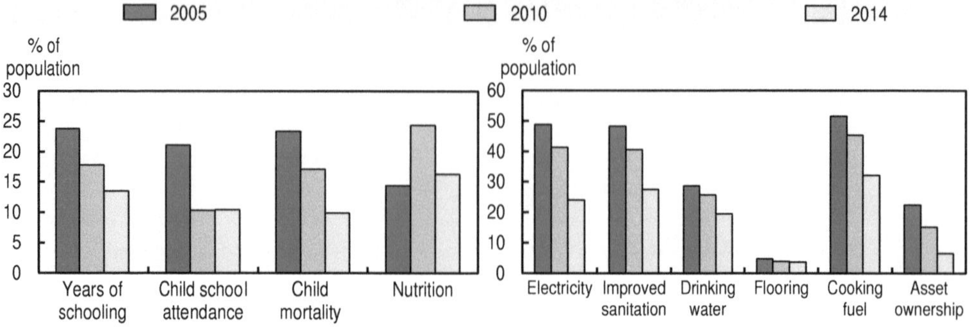

Source: Authors' own calculations based on NIS, Ministry of Health, Cambodia (MoH) and ICF International (2015), *Cambodia Demographic Health Survey 2014*, available at *dhsprogram.com/publications/publication-fr312-dhs-final-reports.cfm*; NIS, MoH and ICF Macro (2011), *Cambodia Demographic Health Survey 2010*, available at *dhsprogram.com/publications/publication-FR249-DHS-Final-Reports.cfm*; and National Institute of Public Health, NIS and Opinion Research Company Macro (2006), *Cambodia Demographic Health Survey 2005*, available at *dhsprogram.com/publications/publication-FR185-DHS-Final-Reports.cfm*.

Non-income poverty is concentrated in rural parts of Cambodia. The multi-dimensional poverty rate is 39% in rural parts but is one-seventh of that level in urban regions. This disparity reflects a lack of access to adequate sanitation, health and education facilities in remote parts of Cambodia, with households often deprived in all these dimensions at once. It also demonstrates that the monetary poverty reduction witnessed since 2004 has not necessarily translated into improvements in living standards or addressed some of the major life cycle risks discussed below.

The provinces with the highest poverty rate in monetary terms in 2014 did not necessarily have the highest prevalence of multi-dimensional poverty and vice versa (Figure 1.9). Households in Phnom Penh fare well relative to other regions in terms of multi-dimensional poverty, even though the rapid growth of the capital is causing severe infrastructural problems (some 34% of housing is in informal settlements). Provinces surrounding Phnom Penh also have lower poverty rates than the rest of the country. Multi-dimensional poverty rates are highest in the mountain and plateau areas in districts close to borders with Thailand and Lao PDR in the north and northeast and Viet Nam in the east.

The rapid decline in monetary poverty has also not been matched by the rate at which subjective well-being indicators have improved. In 2012, Cambodia ranked worst in the world in terms of the percentage of the population thriving (3%, in comparison with a median of 20% in Asia) and third worst in the world in suffering, with 34% rating their quality of life as extremely low, up from 26% in 2011 (Gallup, 2012). More recently, however, there have been signs of improvement. Gallup data for 2015 indicated that more individuals have experienced an improvement in their life situations (Figure 1.10).

Figure 1.9. **Monetary poverty has fallen but multi-dimensional poverty persists**

Monetary poverty rates and multi-dimensional headcount poverty rates by region in Cambodia (2014)

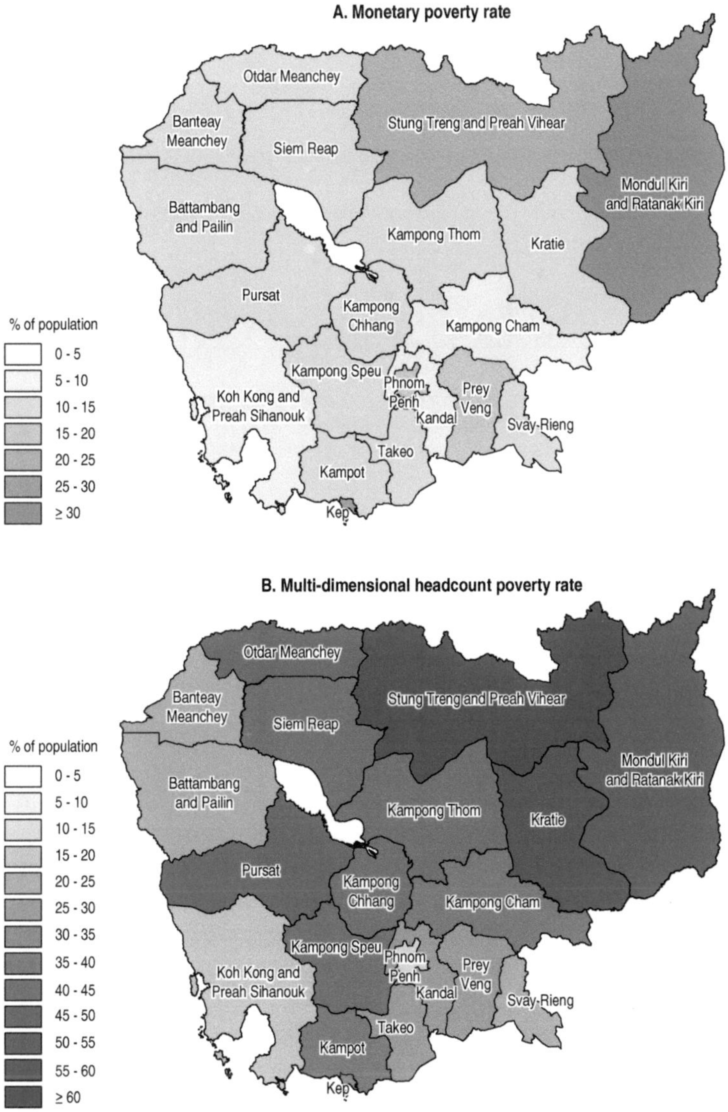

Source: NIS, MoH and ICF International (2015), *Cambodia Demographic Health Survey 2014*, available at *dhsprogram.com/publications/publication-fr312-dhs-final-reports.cfm*; and Oxford Poverty and Human Development Initiative [OPHI] (2016).

Figure 1.10. **A majority of Cambodians report rising living standards**

Evolution of self-reported standard of living in Cambodia (2006-15)

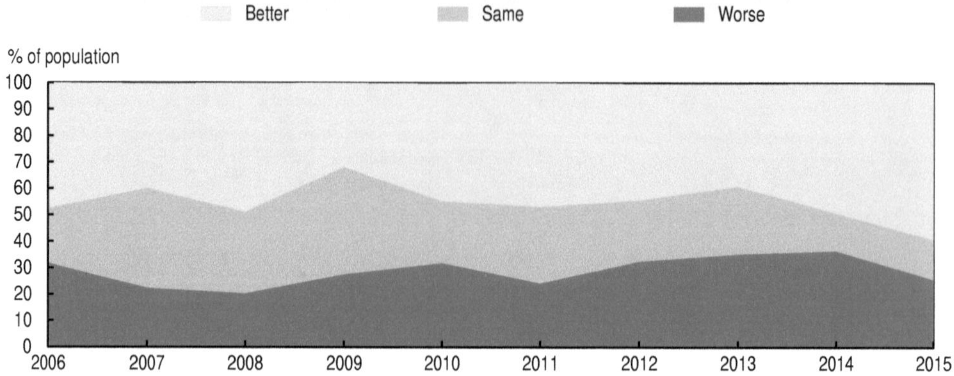

Note: The categories correspond to answers to the following question: "Right now, do you feel your standard of living is getting better or getting worse? Getting better/The same/Getting worse".

Source: Gallup (2016), *Gallup World Poll* (dataset), available at *gallup.com/services/170945/world-poll.aspx*.

Risks affect all stages of the lifecycle

Households confront different risks at different stages in the life cycle of its members. Understanding these risks is essential for tailoring social protection provision to the needs of population and anticipating future demands. Monitoring risks throughout the life cycle is also important, as risks experienced at one age can increase susceptibility to other risks at a later age. Childhood malnutrition, for example, increases the likelihood of low educational outcomes or poor health later in life.

Investment in social protection (and other) policies targeting life cycle stages should be appraised not only against their immediate impact but also with reference to their long-term benefits in safeguarding against risks later in life. By investing in the human capital of today's youth, the RGC not only reduces the extent to which this cohort requires support during their working years but also enhances their future contribution to the economy, thereby ensuring the current demographic dividend is sustained (Box 1.5). Figure 1.11 shows a number of risks for which information is available from the 2014 CSES, as well as their incidence at different ages.

Protecting mothers and children

Maternal and child mortality remain high, despite significant improvements. The number of maternal deaths per thousand live births in Cambodia is high relative to other countries in the region, despite an almost threefold decline between 2000 and 2014 (from 484 to 167) (World Bank, 2016). The Philippines (117), Indonesia (133), Viet Nam (54) and Thailand (20) all performed better than Cambodia; only Lao PDR (197) has a higher rate. Although declining since 2000, infant mortality was 41 deaths per 1 000 live births in 2014 – lower than Lao PDR (51) but higher than Indonesia (23), the Philippines (22), Viet Nam and Thailand (11). The child mortality rate in rural areas is more than twice that in urban areas.

Figure 1.11. **Risks are distributed across the life cycle**

Poverty risks by age in Cambodia (2014)

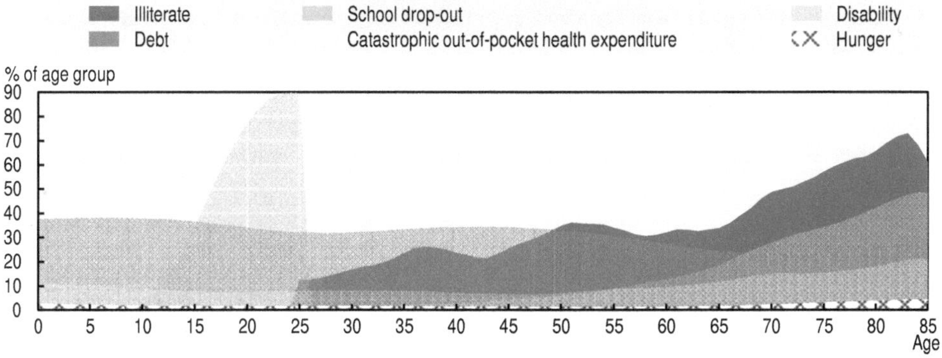

Source: Authors' calculations based on NIS (2004, 2009 and 2014), *Cambodia Socio-Economic Surveys* and Cambodia DHS databases, available at *nada-nis.gov.kh/index.php/catalog/CSES* and *dhsprogram.com/publications/publication-fr312-dhs-final-reports.cfm*.

Communicable diseases, maternal and neonatal disorders are the top causes of infant deaths, followed by water-borne and infectious diseases (Institute for Health Metrics and Evaluation [IHME], 2013). Clean water and proper sanitation, preventive measures and adequate awareness can significantly reduce the mortality burden. The RGC needs to continue efforts to expand childhood immunisation, which is low by regional standards. Basic immunisation coverage was 86% in 2014, a figure which dropped to 60.9% for the lowest household consumption quintile. Using the third dose of the polio vaccine as a proxy, Cambodia's rate of coverage in 2015 (77%) was low by regional standards (United Nations Children's Fund [UNICEF], 2015).

Children in work and out of school

Cambodia's enrolment rates have improved but completion rates remain alarmingly low at each educational level. Figure 1.12 illustrates that, while enrolment in each cycle increased from 2004 to 2014, a dramatic decline from one cycle to the next persisted. According to CSES data, net enrolment in primary school (children aged 6-11) rose from 77% in 2004 to 85% in 2014. Enrolment was 40% for lower secondary, 20% for upper secondary and 12% for tertiary in 2014. Moreover, only 40% of those enrolled in lower secondary and only 20% in upper secondary were expected to complete the respective cycle in 2014/15 (Ministry of Education, Youth and Sport [MoEYS], 2015).

Box 1.2. **Nutrition levels remain a major concern**

According to the International Food Policy Research Institute (IFPRI) Global Hunger Index for 2015, Cambodia achieved the largest reduction in hunger levels of any country between 2000 and 2015 (von Grebmer et al, 2015). However, IFPRI still classifies Cambodia as a country with a serious hunger situation. The indicators for children are particularly worrying: 32% of children experienced stunting in Cambodia in 2014, 24% of children were underweight, and 10% of children under age 5 experienced wasting (an increase from 2005) (NIS, MoH, and ICF International, 2015).

Poor nutritional outcomes are not associated only with poor households. DHS data for 2014 show that 20% of children under the age of 5 in the eighth decile of the income distribution are underweight, versus 35% in the first decile, while 26% of children in the same age group were stunted in the eighth decile, versus 43% in the first decile.

A 2013 study estimated that approximately 30% of infant deaths between 2013 and 2023 will be linked to malnutrition (Council for Agricultural and Rural Development [CARD], UNICEF and United Nations [UN] World Food Programme [WFP], 2013). Aside from the human cost, childhood malnutrition represents an economic burden today and into the future. The same study calculated that the annual losses in potential economic output associated with childhood malnutrition are equivalent to approximately USD 250-400 million or 1.5-2.6% of total annual GDP in 2013. Two-thirds of this amount will be attributable to productivity losses associated with the performance of today's children in tomorrow's labour market.

The RGC's scholarship and school food programmes are key interventions in later childhood. International evidence shows how such programmes not only encourage attendance but also improve children's learning outcomes (Adato and Bassett, 2009; ILO, 2010; Department for International Development [DFID], 2011; Grantham-McGregor et al., 2007; Martorell, 1995; Pollitt et al., 1995). Eligibility for these programmes in Cambodia is determined through the IDPoor targeting system, which means that only children in the lower deciles benefit from the programmes (assuming they are implemented in their district); the incidence of malnutrition higher up the income distribution indicates the shortcomings of targeting such interventions.

In response to the challenge of childhood malnutrition, the RGC has developed the National Strategy for Food Security and Nutrition (NSFSN) (2014-2018). The NSFSN is based on three pillars: i) more productive and diversified agriculture and livestock sectors to increase the availability of and access to food; ii) a focus on the nutrition of mothers and children; and iii) the role social protection can play in improving food security. This multisectoral approach is consistent with the challenge of malnutrition, whose causes include a lack of dietary diversity, lack of access to clean drinking water and sanitation, limited knowledge of basic nutrition, and women's long working days and absence from household decision making (WFP, forthcoming).

Figure 1.12. **Secondary enrolment rates remain low, especially in rural areas**

Net enrolment by cycle and year, and by cycle and region in Cambodia (2004-14)

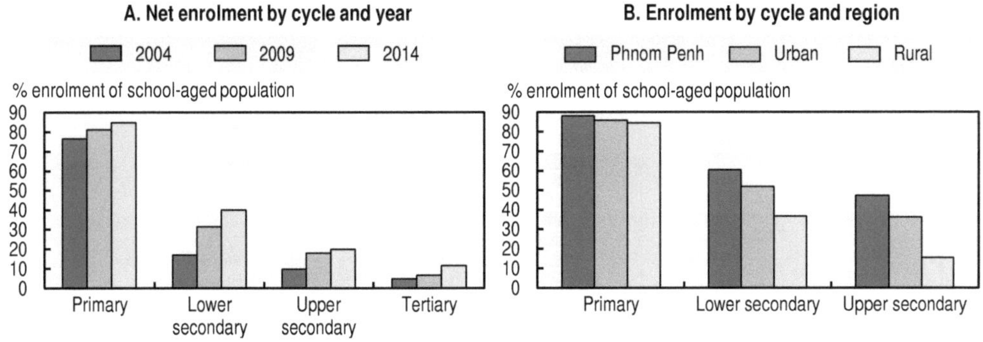

Source: Authors' calculations based on NIS (2004, 2009 and 2014), *Cambodia Socio-Economic Surveys*, available at *nada-nis.gov.kh/index.php/catalog/CSES*.

Primary enrolment rates are similar for rural areas, urban areas and Phnom Penh, but enrolment and completion rates for lower and upper secondary are much higher in urban areas than in rural. In 2014, rural drop-out rates were 9.1% for primary education, 22% for lower secondary and 15% for upper secondary, compared with 6.5%, 11% and 6.7% for the urban population, respectively (United States Agency for International Development [USAID], 2011). The low enrolment rates and high drop-out rates largely reflect the direct and indirect costs (such as foregone labour income) of allowing children to attend school. Cambodia's scholarship programmes can offset these costs, especially if education is perceived as a means of improving a child's long-term employment prospects.

Child employment is declining but remains commonplace. According to the 2014 CSES, 30% of individuals under 18 not in school cited the need to contribute to household income as the reason for non-attendance. Another 12.5% said they were too poor to attend and 6.6% said they were needed to help with household chores. According to the International Labour Organization (ILO) and the National Institute of Statistics, Cambodia (NIS), 19.1% of children aged 5-17 participated in the labour force in 2012, of whom 50.7% were girls, 37.0% were younger than 15 years old, and 86.7% lived in rural areas (ILO and NIS, 2013).

By the RGC's definitions, 56.9% of children participating in the labour force were classified as child labourers, among whom 31.3% were engaged in hazardous labour (ILO and NIS, 2013). Figure 1.13 shows a decline in child employment between 2004 and 2014, which was especially pronounced between 2009 and 2014 and among younger age groups. Still, among those aged 15-17, more than 50% participated in the labour force in 2014.

Figure 1.13. **Child employment is decreasing**
Child employment by age group in Cambodia (2004-14)

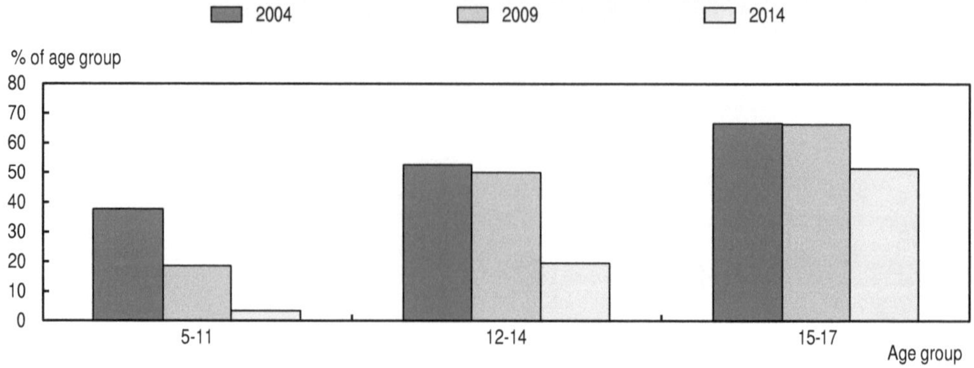

Source: Authors' calculations based on NIS (2004, 2009 and 2014), *Cambodia Socio-Economic Surveys*, available at *nada-nis.gov.kh/index.php/catalog/CSES*.

Labour force participation among youth is declining

In 2013, 74.5% of males and 68.1% of females aged 15-24 participated in the labour force, down from 77.5% and 74.2% in 2009, respectively. This suggests that young people, especially women, are staying in school longer. However, the decline may also reflect a mismatch between young people's skills and labour market requirements (ADB and ILO, 2015). Figure 1.14 shows that literacy rates have improved over the past decade yet Cambodia still has the lowest adult literacy rate in SEA (United Nations Educational, Scientific and Cultural Organization [UNESCO], 2016).

Figure 1.14. **Literacy rates are increasing**
Literacy rates by age in Cambodia (2004-14)

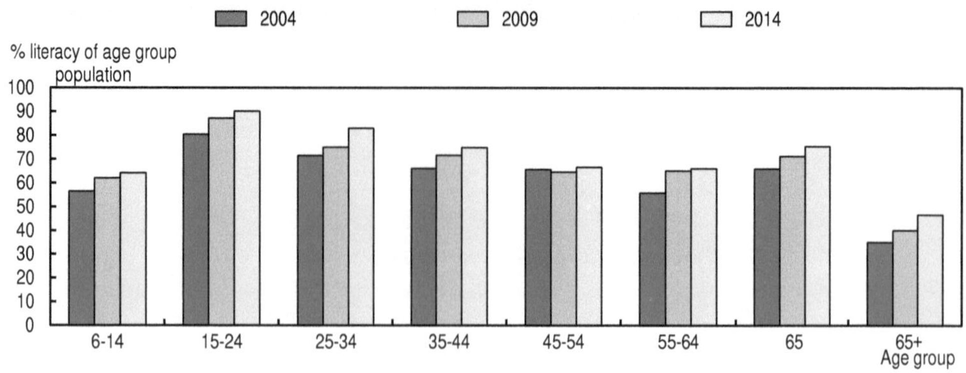

Source: Authors' calculations based on NIS (2004, 2009 and 2014), *Cambodia Socio-Economic Surveys*, available at *nada-nis.gov.kh/index.php/catalog/CSES*.

Low enrolment and poor educational quality, especially at the secondary level, has been cited as a possible reason as to why some 42.5% of young workers underperform in their jobs (ADB and ILO, 2015). These factors also have negative implications for Cambodia's international competitiveness. A lack of education also lowers both the quality of jobs individuals can attain and their long-term income prospects. According to the 2014 CSES, 16% of individuals with five years of education were poor, compared with 3% of those with 15 years of education.

Cambodia's technical vocational education and training programmes give a second chance to workers who did not complete secondary school. They have a key role to play in improving the productivity of such groups, who typically end up in low-skilled jobs in the informal sector. As Chapter 2 identifies, these programmes are currently not rolled out broadly enough to match the scale of the challenge.

The rate of employment is high but wages are often low

Cambodia's unemployment rate was below 3% in 2015, while the level of labour force participation is among the highest in the world. According to 2014 CSES data, participation was 77.5% for women and 87.9% for men. However, Cambodia has one of the highest levels of working poor in the world. More than half of the employed population earns less than the USD 2 per day upper poverty line. The average rate of poverty by this benchmark for wage employees is 56.5%, not far below the 65.8% rate for own-account or unpaid family workers (ILO, 2013).

Low-paid work and excessive hours are prevalent in Cambodia. The rate of low-wage work (defined as earning less than two-thirds the median wage) was over 30% for the working age population (NIS, 2014). This explains the prevalence of the "working poor" in the LCA. As Figure 1.15 shows, low-wage work is most prevalent in the 18-24 age group. In addition, low-wage earners are concentrated in rural regions (15% versus only 5% in Phnom Penh).

Figure 1.15. **Low-wage work is highest for women and men in the 18-24 age cohort**

Low-wage work by age and gender in Cambodia (2014)

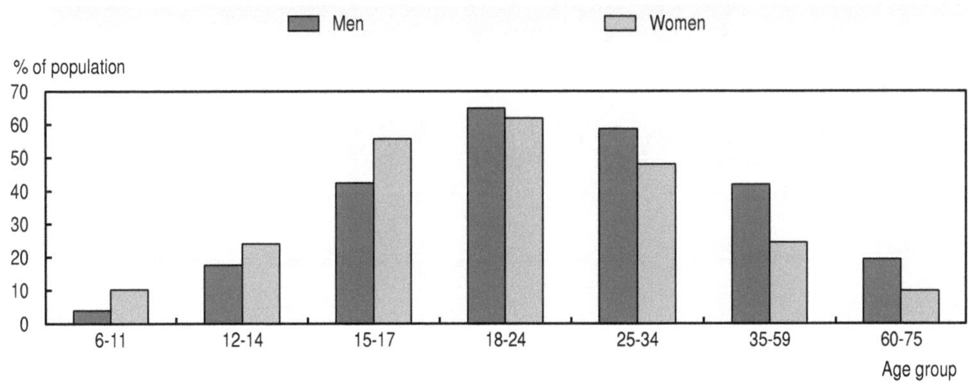

Source: Authors' calculations based on NIS (2014), *Cambodia Socio-Economic Survey 2014*, available at *nada-nis.gov.kh/index.php/catalog/CSES*.

The proportion of the labour force working excessive hours (defined by the Labour Law [1997] as more than 48 hours per week) exceeds 40% across all age groups and rises with age for cohorts aged above 24 (Figure 1.16). According to a survey conducted by the RGC and the ILO, 49.6% of Cambodia's 7.2 million employed persons worked more than 48 hours per week in 2012 (ILO and NIS, 2013). This phenomenon affected child workers and older persons more than those in middle age groups and was more common in urban regions (59%) than rural (52%).

Figure 1.16. **A majority of the workforce works excessive hours**

Excessive work hours by age in Cambodia (2004-14)

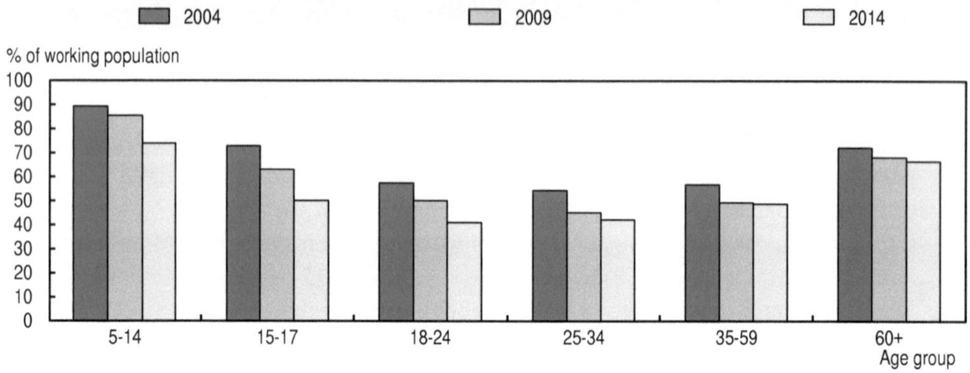

Source: Authors' calculations based on NIS (2004, 2009 and 2014), *Cambodia Socio-Economic Surveys*, available at *nada-nis.gov.kh/index.php/catalog/CSES*.

The rate of vulnerable employment – own-account or unpaid family labour – has decreased since 2004 but 58% of labour force participation is still classified as vulnerable (NIS, 2014). The youngest and oldest workers are the groups most exposed to vulnerable labour, and rural workers are more vulnerable than those living in urban areas (70% in rural regions versus 29% in Phnom Penh). This rural contingent includes family members working in unpaid farm jobs who are highly dependent on seasonal and uncertain household income.

A 10-percentage-point difference between labour force participation among men and women has persisted since at least 1990, even though women have been at the forefront of the structural transformation of the economy and employment due to the sex-selective employment practices of the garment factories (ILO, 2012). The 2014 CSES indicates a pay gap of 35% between men and women workers. This is an improvement from a decade earlier but Cambodia remains one of the worst performers in SEA in this respect. Women are more likely to be in low-paid and vulnerable employment. Employers prefer to provide short-term contracts that do not oblige them to pay maternity benefits and are reluctant to pay for childcare services (Human Rights Watch, 2015). The unpaid work gap in Cambodia is 3.5 hours per day (ADB, 2013).

The proportion of the total workforce in wage employment (formal or informal) has more than doubled, from 15.8% in 2000 to 35.8% in 2012 (ILO, 2015). However, informal employment is still the norm across the workforce, making it difficult to expand coverage of social insurance given that existing contributory arrangements are accessible only by those in formal employment. According to the 2012 Labour Force Survey, just 8.6% of men and 4.1% of women aged 15 or over were formally employed outside the agricultural sector, while 57.6% of men and 63.2% of women worked in the informal sector (ILO and NIS, 2013).

The high level of informality relates in part to the fact that the majority of businesses are smaller (in staff terms) than the minimum threshold for registration based on the Labour Law, which is generally interpreted to be a headcount of eight. In 2011, micro, small and medium-sized enterprises accounted for 73% of all paid employment in Cambodia and 99.8% of businesses; 97% of these were unregistered (ADB and ILO, 2015). Of total informal employment in 2011, 28.2% was in manufacturing, of which around 50% was in the garment and footwear sector and 11% in construction.

Box 1.3. **Improving conditions for garment workers**

Employment in the garment and footwear sector has increased rapidly, from just under 200 000 people in 2000 to 605 000 in 2016 (ILO, 2017). The advancement of rights for these workers has been integral to the development of this sector, which is a cornerstone of the economy.

Through the US-Cambodia Bilateral Textile Agreement signed in 1999, the United States increased the quotas for Cambodian garments upon improved compliance with conditions related to labour market standards. The International Labour Organization (ILO) has been closely involved in monitoring these improvements since 2001 through the Better Factories Cambodia (BFC) initiative, which was maintained even after the agreement expired (Asuyama and Neou, 2012; UNDP, 2016).

The garment and footwear sector is the only sector in which the minimum wage prescribed by Cambodia's Labour Law prevails (ILO, 2016). The minimum wage has increased ad hoc since first established in accordance with the Labour Law (1997). It did not keep up with inflation between 2000 and 2012, rising from USD 45 to USD 61 per month over that period (in nominal terms), but it has increased sharply since.

The minimum wage for 2016 was set at USD 140 per month, which was marginally above the poverty line (ILO, 2016). For 2017, it was increased to USD 153 per month (ILO, 2017). With effect from January 2017, the RGC also increased the lower income tax threshold from USD 200 to USD 250 per month, which ensured that the majority of garment workers were exempt, and it also introduced allowances for transport and accommodation for workers in the sector, along with rent and utility-rate controls.

Box 1.3. **Improving conditions for garment workers** *(cont.)*

Although low wages are intrinsic to Cambodia's competitiveness, these changes have not (yet) had an adverse impact on the sector. Cambodia's share of the global market for garment and footwear exports has risen from 0.7% in 2005 to 1.5% in 2015 (ILO, 2016), while exports rose by 10.7% on-year in 2014, 14.5% in 2015 and 7.2% in 2016.

Nor are employment levels thought to have suffered as a result of increased wages. Employment in the garment and footwear sector grew by 18.6% on-year in 2013, 13.5% in 2014 and 10.4% in 2015 (ILO, 2016). Although employment then declined by 2.9% in 2016, this is thought to have been due to changes in the methodology for calculating these figures.

The growth of the garment and footwear sector is a mixed blessing for workers' rights. The rapid growth of the sector has exceeded the RGC's ability to monitor and enforce the regulations governing working conditions across the sector, as prescribed by Cambodia's Labour Law (1997) (Human Rights Watch, 2015; RGC, 1997). While the BFC initiative plays a crucial role in supporting the RGC in monitoring garment factories, it lacks enforcement powers and focuses mostly on factories for export (Human Rights Watch, 2015). Union representation in the garment sector is patchy. In 2014, 29% of factories surveyed had no union representation at all (Human Rights Watch, 2015).

However, the provision of social protection for workers in the garment and footwear sector is improving significantly. They now have access to employment injury insurance and health insurance through the National Social Security Fund (NSSF), as will be discussed in Chapter 2. Moreover, the NSSF has a mandate to inspect factories to ensure that they are complying with social security regulations and other legislations, which bolsters the RGC's overall inspection and monitoring capacity.

Disability and old age

Disability affects Cambodians throughout the life cycle. According to the 2014 CSES, 4% of the population was affected by a disability in 2014,[4] the most common being moving and hearing difficulties. The main causes of these impairments are old age, disease and congenital disorders, although 4.2% attributed their disability to land mines and 2.6% were suffering from a disability related to war. Figure 1.17 shows the incidence of different disabilities at different ages. Up to age 14, children are most likely to suffer psychological difficulties which gradually become more prominent throughout childhood and early adulthood, peaking between the ages of 35 and 59.

Living with a disability in Cambodia is associated with increased risk of poverty. For households with one or more disabled member, 18.2% were below the poverty line, compared with 12.8% for those with none (NIS, 2014). The literacy rate among the disabled is only 46%, compared with 78% nationally, which may indicate a lack of special education services. Moreover, the lack of such skills may reduce their opportunities to enter the labour force. 60% of persons with disabilities could not perform any income-generating activity (NIS, 2014), putting them at high risk of monetary poverty. Without access to specialised education or work opportunities, persons with disabilities are dependent on other members of their households, which severely strains household resources, especially in the absence of a public disability benefit.

Figure 1.17. **Types of disability vary across the lifecycle**

Incidence of disability by age group in Cambodia (2014)

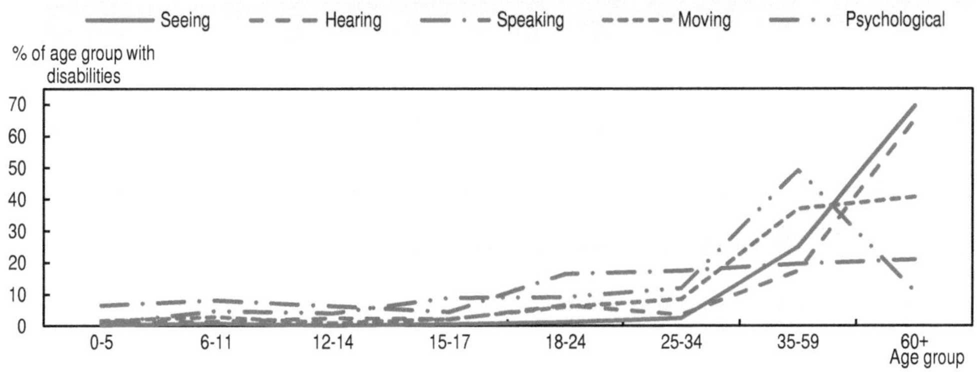

Source: Authors' calculations based on NIS (2014), *Cambodia Socio-Economic Survey 2014*.

The elderly population, on the other hand, appears to be at lesser risk of falling into poverty than the population as a whole. Some 10.5% of individuals aged 60-69 are living below the national monetary poverty line, rising to 13.3% for those aged 70-79 (NIS, 2014). While family support might be an important reason for this, many elderly people appear to have no option but to work: according to 2014 CSES, 27% of individuals aged 65 and over participated in the labour force, of whom 86% were engaged in vulnerable employment and 72% worked excessive hours. In both cases, these rates are higher than the working-age average. The health consequences of unsafe labour conditions can be especially acute for the elderly, for whom average health care costs are nearly four times higher than for children (Ministry of Health [MoH], 2007).

A reliance on informal assistance networks to support the elderly will be problematic as the population ages. In the absence of a social pension and with limited coverage of contributory retirement schemes (discussed in Chapter 2), the low level of poverty among elderly individuals indicates that family and other social networks make a major contribution to ensuring the well-being of those over 60. As the population ages, these informal arrangements will come under strain, since there will be fewer workers to support a greater number of elderly people. Internal migration also disrupts resource-sharing among families (OECD, 2017).

Debt

Household debt is endemic among certain populations in Cambodia. Ovesen, Trankell and Öjendal (1996) note that "indebtedness and usury have long been recognised as major problems for Cambodia's peasants". The nature of indebtedness has changed with the expansion of the formal financial sector, in particular microfinance institutions. The number of individuals borrowing from such institutions rose from 50 000 to 1.1 million between 1995 and 2012, over which period the amount of outstanding loans increased from USD 3 million to USD 732 million (Liv, 2013). The University of Zurich's Over-indebtedness Index classifies Cambodia as a high-risk country due to the absence of a regulatory framework to manage the rapid expansion of the microfinance system (Kappel, Krauss and Lontzek, 2010).

Debt incidence has declined gradually since 2000 but remains high in rural areas. Figure 1.18 shows the decline in debt levels between 2004 and 2014, as well as the debt incidence. Approximately one-third of households in each of the first seven consumption deciles were in debt in 2014. Across the distribution, the number of households in debt decreased from 43% to 31% between 2004 and 2014, but the average amount of outstanding loans per household in the same period increased from KHR 993 000 to KHR 4.3 million (Kappel, Krauss and Lontzek, 2010). Multiple loans can compound indebtedness. A 2013 survey of 1 500 borrowers from microfinance institutions showed 28% had two loans, 13% had three loans, 15% had more than four loans, and only 56% were solvent (Liv, 2013). 2014 CSES data showed 35% of rural households are in debt, compared with 10% in Phnom Penh and 29% in other urban regions.

Figure 1.18. **Household debt is highest among the poor and vulnerable**

Household debt by consumption decile in Cambodia (2004-14)

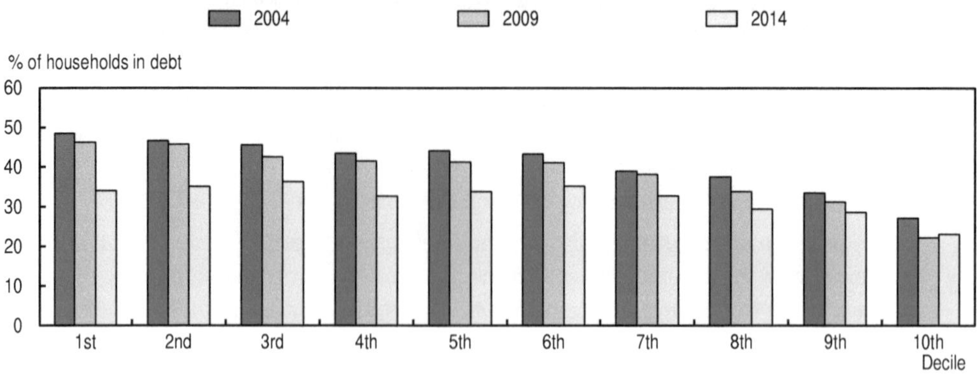

Note: The deciles of household consumption in 2014 Cambodian riel (KHR) are defined according to the following cut-offs: 350 282 / 456 077 / 549 250 / 636 399 / 729 553 / 829 604 / 961 286 / 1 137 181 / 1 495 614.

Source: Authors' calculations based on NIS (2004, 2009 and 2014), Cambodia Socio-Economic Surveys, available at *nada-nis.gov.kh/index.php/catalog/CSES*.

Figure 1.19 shows how borrowing for consumption declined significantly between the 2004 and 2014 CSES but remains relatively high (NIS, 2014). Poor households are more likely to i) borrow from informal moneylenders; ii) have a high ratio of outstanding debt to average annual per capita consumption; and iii) borrow for subsistence purposes, such as consumption, medical expenses, cultural and religious ceremonies or servicing existing debts (ADB, 2014). A significant number of households who have relied on loans to increase their consumption above the poverty line risk falling back into poverty when they have to repay their debts.

Figure 1.19. **Households are borrowing less for consumption and more for asset building**

Reasons for household borrowing in Cambodia (2004-14)

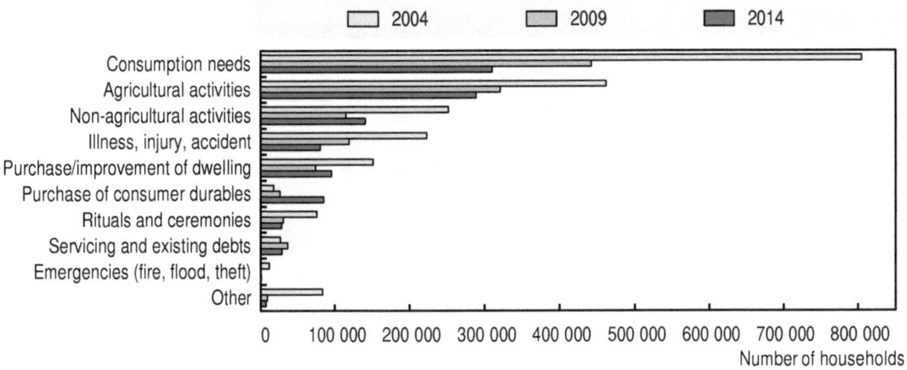

Source: Authors' calculations based on NIS (2004, 2009 and 2014), *Cambodia Socio-Economic Surveys*, available at *nada-nis.gov.kh/index.php/catalog/CSES*.

Cambodia's economy is in transition but needs to diversify further

The composition of GDP and employment has changed significantly since 2000 (Figure 1.20) (World Bank, 2015a). The contribution of agriculture to GDP fell from 37.8% in 2000 to 30.4% in 2014, while industry's contribution grew from 23.0% to 27.0%, reflecting not only the rapid development of the textile sector, which barely existed before the 1990s, but also growth in construction. The service sector remains the largest contributor to GDP at 42.6% in 2014 and is being sustained by strong growth in tourism. However, gains in agricultural productivity have been an important driver of growth: as the World Bank recently reported, "Cambodian agriculture is in the midst of rapidly transitioning from a traditional subsistence to a modern commercial sector" (World Bank, 2015b). From 2000 to 2015, employment in agriculture fell from 73.7% of the workforce to 52.7%; employment in the industrial sector almost doubled, from 8.4% to 16.7%; and employment in services rose from 17.9% to 30.6% (ILO, 2015).

Figure 1.20. **The structure of the economy is changing but agriculture remains dominant**

Composition of employment and economic sectors in Cambodia, % of GDP (2000-15)

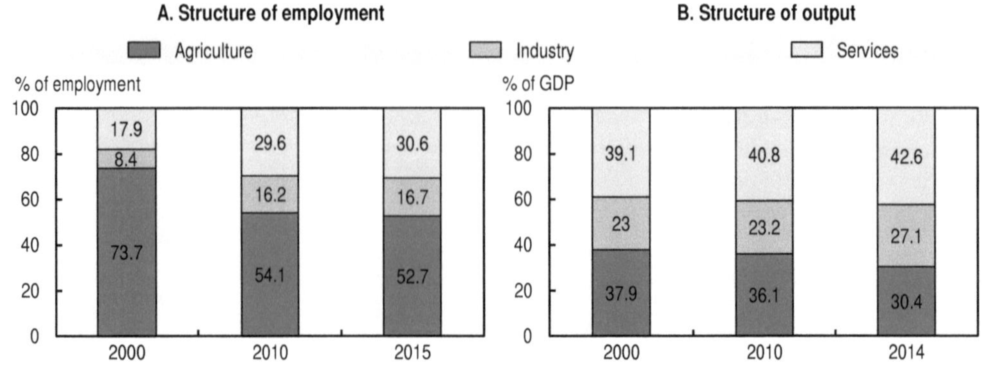

Note: GDP units are in PPP constant 2011 international US dollars.

Source: World Bank (2015a), *World Development Indicators* (database), available at *data.worldbank.org/products/wdi.*

From 2000 to 2015, employment in agriculture fell from 73.7% of the workforce to 52.7%. Over the same period, employment in the industrial sector almost doubled, from 8.4% to 16.7% and employment in services rose from 17.9% to 30.6% (Figure 1.20). The movement of labour out of agriculture is typically associated with a decrease in household and own-account work into wage employment. However, as noted above, formal employment has not increased dramatically in Cambodia.

Robust growth and structural transformation are expected to continue. Long-term projections of population growth and productivity indicate an average annual growth rate of close to 6% between 2020 and 2050. Based on the economic dynamics of the past 15 years, agriculture will contribute just 15% to GDP and employ 42% of the working-age population by 2050,[5] while industry and services combined will contribute 85% to GDP and employ 58% of the workforce (see Annex 1.A2 for a description of the methodology used to derive these forecasts).

Cambodia's output per worker is expected to increase by 261% between 2000 and 2020, the fastest growth in the region after Lao PDR and Myanmar. However, as Figure 1.21 shows, Cambodia's level of productivity lags behind that of its neighbours in SEA (ILO, 2015).

Cambodia's garment and footwear exporters face strong competition from other producers, in particular those in Bangladesh and Viet Nam. In addition, Cambodia is heavily reliant on exports to the European Union, the United States and Canada, while exports to Japan have also grown recently (ILO, 2017). A slowdown in these key markets has an immediate impact on growth in the broader economy, as occurred in 2009.

Figure 1.21. **Productivity is rising but remains low by regional standards**

Output per worker across select SEA countries (2000-20)

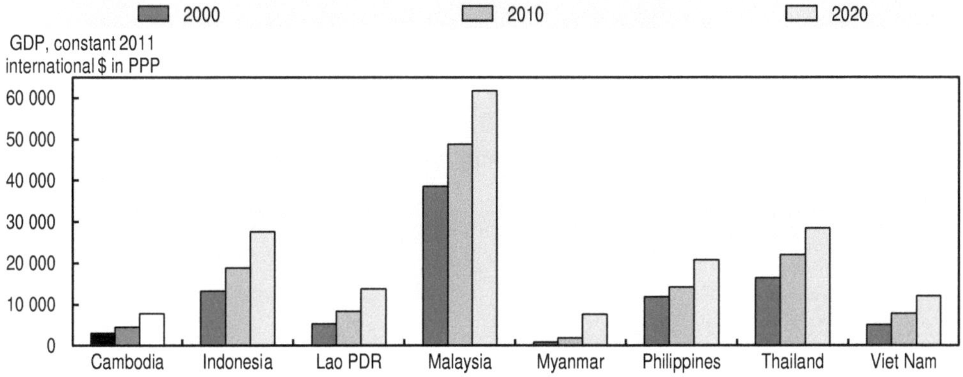

Source: ILO (2015), *Key Indicators of the Labour Market* (database), available at *ilo.org/global/statistics-and-databases/research-and-databases/kilm/lang--en/index.htm.*

Meanwhile, declining export prices have forced the sector to continually increase production with new factories and more manpower. However, this model cannot be sustained indefinitely, due to a limited supply of young (especially female) rural workers who can join the manufacturing sector (ADB and ILO, 2015). Cambodia's recent graduation to lower-middle income status could reduce access to key markets: the Everything but Arms (EBA) trade arrangement with the European Union provides preferential access to exports from lower-income and least developed countries.

Looking ahead, automation poses a huge threat to Cambodia's garment and footwear industry, in particular employment in the sector. The ILO calculates that 88% of workers in Cambodia's garment sector are at risk from automation (Chang and Huyen, 2016). Given that such workers comprise such a large share of the formal workforce, Cambodia ranks high among the countries in SEA most vulnerable to the fourth industrial revolution.

Meanwhile, resource constraints and climate change threaten the continued growth of the rural sector. Substantial increases in the area under cultivation – an important contributor to growth in the agriculture sector between 2002 and 2012 – will not be sustained into the future (World Bank, 2014b). There is also a shortage of manpower, with only 1.6 workers per hectare, a level typical in countries with highly mechanised agriculture sectors (World Bank, 2014b). While the labour shortage has driven up rural wages, it is a major concern for future productivity and underscores the need for mechanisation. Moreover, Cambodia is one of the countries at greatest risk from climate change, which directly threatens rural livelihoods and coastal tourism (Box 1.4).

Box 1.4. **Climate change poses risks for Cambodia**

Cambodia's agriculture sector is highly vulnerable to climate change. Research shows that a 1°C increase in minimum temperatures during the dry season reduces rice yields by 10% (Peng et al., 2004).[7] For subsistence farmers, loss of income in the event of crop failure is compounded by food shortages.

Climate change also threatens livelihoods in coastal areas exposed to rising sea levels and increased typhoon activity (RGC, 2013). Although tourism is starting to play a greater role in the coastal economy, households in these areas derive their incomes mainly from agriculture and fisheries. These low-lying terrains are increasingly prone to climate change-related storm surges, floods and rising sea levels (Cambodia Climate Change Alliance [CCCA], 2012).

More than half of Cambodians depend on the agriculture sector for their livelihoods. Any disastrous climate effect (flooding, drought) or non-disastrous climate effect (changing rainfall patterns, cyclical droughts) can exacerbate food insecurity for these households. A lack of support in the case of non-disastrous climate-related effects can perpetuate poverty traps and increase the risk of households near poverty falling back into poverty.

A 2015 World Bank report on the impact of climate change on poverty identified the central role of micro-insurance in protecting low-income individuals (Fay et al., 2015). A report on micro-insurance in Cambodia found two principal sources of climate change-related risk: ill-health/injury and crop failure due to drought and floods (UNDP, 2013b). While Health Equity Funds cover a large number of poor households against health risks, there are no formal arrangements, public or private, insuring against crop failure.

The principal risk-mitigation strategy is for Cambodians to save against climate events; when savings are exhausted, they borrow (UNDP, 2013b). Of 390 households surveyed soon after the floods that affected 18 of 24 provinces in 2011, 48% had to take a loan as a direct consequence. Some 60% of respondents subsequently experienced difficulty in repaying their loans, with annual interest rates estimated to be as high as 65% (Bullen and Corita, 2012).

A study of SEA households found that those with higher incomes take more proactive measures in response to climate change versus the reactive responses of poorer households (Francisco et al., 2011). Ex post responses, such as evacuation or emergency support, often come at a cost to the RGC. Moreover, coping strategies involving borrowing, reduced food consumption or taking children out of school can cause households to suffer significant long-term costs. Social protection can enhance long-term resilience to climate change by providing resources for productive investments in land and diversification of agricultural activities. The cost of a social protection programme that facilitates proactive measures is more than offset in economy-wide savings (Fay et al., 2015).

Box 1.4. **Climate change poses risks for Cambodia** *(cont.)*

In 2013, the RGC published the Cambodia Climate Change Strategic Plan (CCCSP) for 2014-23 (RGC, 2013). The CCCSP identifies a role for adaptive social protection in mitigating the impact of climate change, but it is not yet clear what this will entail. A social protection programme that can be scaled up rapidly to mitigate anticipated impacts of climate change – be it drought or flood – is an important complement to interventions that enhance the long-term resilience of households.

Cambodia's narrow economic base, low productivity, rising real wages and ageing population could combine to constrain its long-term growth prospects. The Industrial Development Policy (2015-2025) recognises the importance of establishing a broader economic base and aims to reduce the proportion of garment and footwear exports from close to 80% of total exports to 50% by 2025, with other manufactured goods and processed agricultural products filling the gap. This process will not be straightforward. The garment industry, which is dominated by foreign-owned firms,[6] has not generated significant linkages to other domestic producers or the technological spill-overs that might have benefited the economy as a whole (UNDP, 2014). As a result, it is not obvious which activities to promote in the industrial sector, how successful these will be in promoting sustained economic growth, or the extent to which they will absorb the continued growth in the working-age population, which is expected to increase by 25% by 2030 (UNDP, 2016).

Demographics are favourable now but the population will age fast in the future

Cambodia's rapid economic growth has coincided with strong but decelerating population growth. Its population grew from 12.2 million in 2000 to 15.7 million in 2016 (UN DESA, 2017), while the total fertility rate and rate of population growth are both declining (Figure 1.22). The total fertility rate declined from 6.9 in 1950-55 to 5.4 in 1975-80, partly as a result of the genocide inflicted by the Khmer Rouge regime between 1975 and 1979. This was followed by a spike in 1980-85, after which fertility rates continued their decline. Between 2015 and 2020, the average fertility rate is projected at 2.5, the third-highest in SEA after Lao PDR and the Philippines. Between 2035 and 2040, it is projected to drop to replacement rate and continue to fall thereafter.

Figure 1.22. **The pace of population growth is slowing**

Population growth and fertility rates (1976-2076)

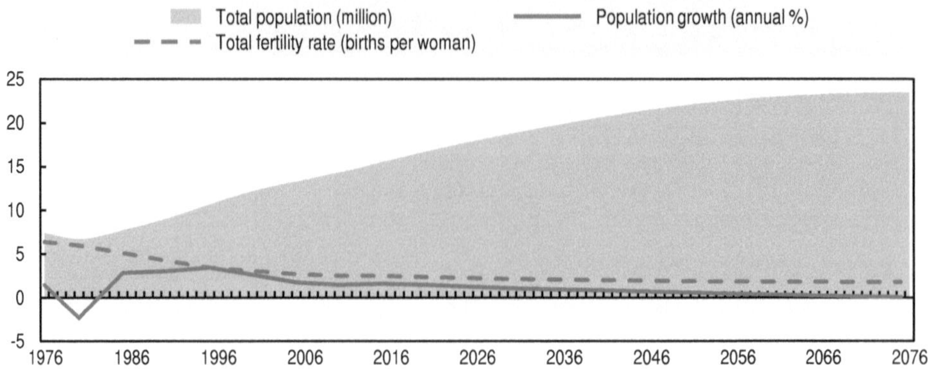

Source: UN DESA (2017), World Population Prospects: The 2017 Revision, available at *un.org/en/development/desa/population/publication.*

Figure 1.23 shows population pyramids from 1976 to 2076. The relatively small cohort aged 35 and above and the relatively large cohort aged 30-34 in 2016 reflect the impact of the Khmer Rouge regime and the baby boom that occurred after its demise. Today's labour force is smaller than it would have been according to the long-term population growth rate but has a sizeable youth bulge. Another legacy of the Khmer Rouge regime and conflicts of that time is an imbalance in the ratio of adult and elderly women to men; the 2008 census showed 42% of women over 60 were widowed, compared with only 10% for men.

Figure 1.24 compares Cambodia's dependency ratio with that of other countries in the region from 1980 to 2100. Up until the mid-1970s, its demographic trends were closely aligned with those of its neighbours but the impact of the Khmer Rouge regime and the subsequent baby boom created a second spike in the dependency ratio between the mid-1980s and around 2000, after which its dependency ratio has been declining to the middle of the distribution. The ratios for Lao PDR and Myanmar are more favourable than Cambodia's.[8] Thailand's dependency ratio was the lowest in 2015 but is projected to rise rapidly to become the highest in the region by 2035 – an important factor in its demand for workers from Cambodia.

The dependency ratio fell from 98% in 2000 to 56% in 2015, when individuals aged 14 and under accounted for 32% of the total population, while those aged 65 and over accounted for 4%. The decline in the dependency ratio and the associated growth of the working-age population is the underlying basis for a demographic dividend, which in turn can lead to major short- and long-term growth benefits (Box 1.5). As fertility rates decline further, the dependency ratio will continue to fall until 2043, at which point the age cohorts born during the baby boom will reach retirement, and the dependency ratio will increase rapidly.

Figure 1.23. **Cambodia's population is beginning to age**

Population pyramids (1976-2076)

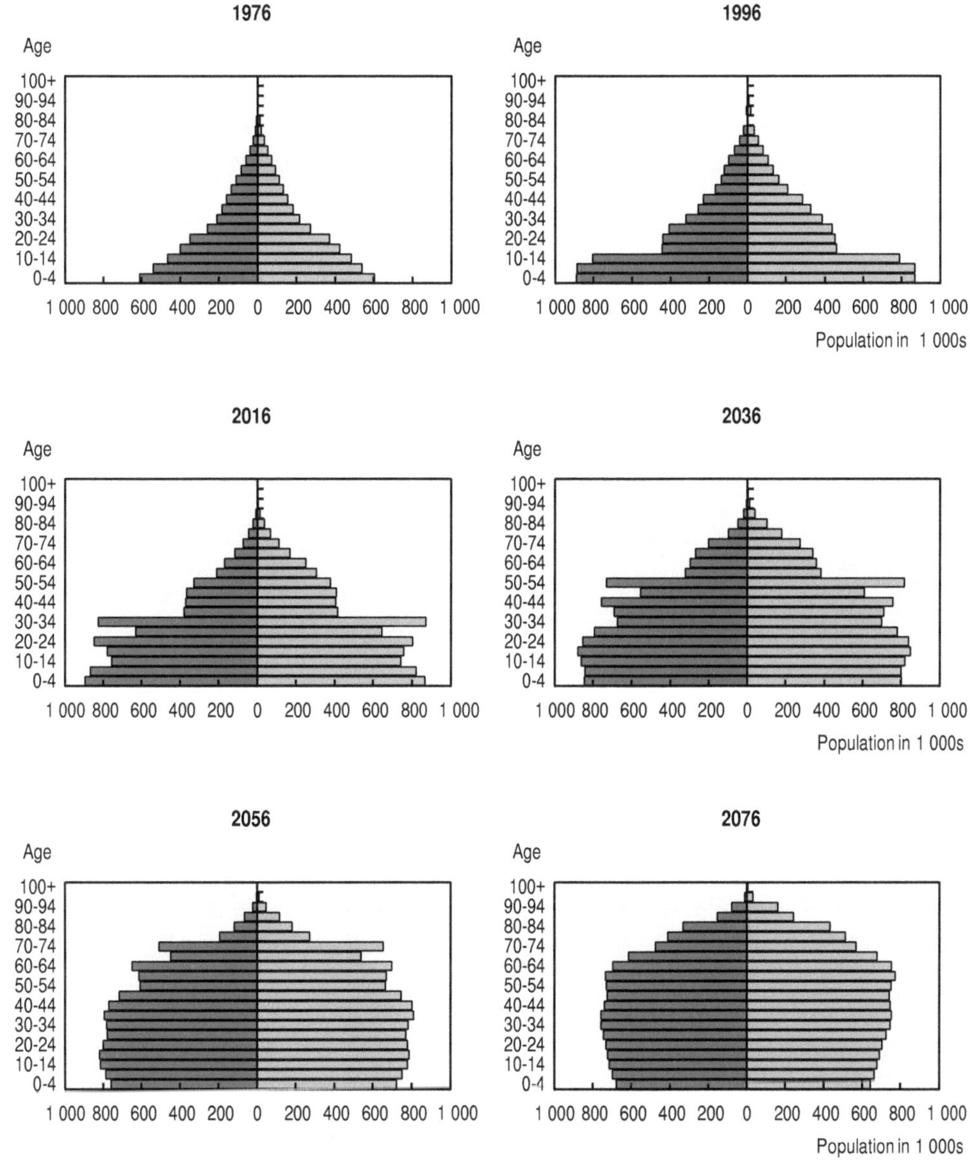

Source: UN DESA (2017), *World Population Prospects: The 2017 Revision*, available at *un.org/en/development/desa/population/publication.*

By 2050, the proportion of individuals aged 14 and under to the working-age population will fall to 22%, while those aged 65 and over will rise to 13%. Ageing of the population will be compounded by rising longevity: life expectancy at birth is projected to rise from 67.6 years in 2015 to 78.8 years in 2050. As the population starts to age, so too will their health needs, with chronic conditions likely to be increasingly important relative to communicable diseases. Over the long term, these changes will have implications for the level of demand for disability benefits and pensions.

Figure 1.24. **Population dynamics will remain favourable**

Dependency ratios in SEA (1980-2100)

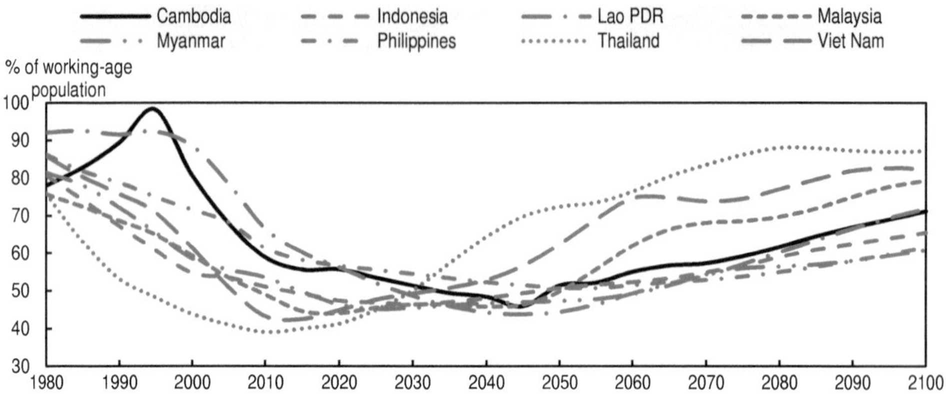

Source: UN DESA (2017), *World Population Prospects: The 2017 Revision*, available at *un.org/en/development/desa/population/publication*.

Rapid growth in international migration has major implications for the size of Cambodia's labour force. Within SEA, only Lao PDR is expected to have a higher emigration rate between 2015 and 2020 (UN DESA, 2015a). The number of Cambodians working abroad is estimated at 1.2 million, or 7.6% of the population, a sharp increase from 3.4% in 2010 (UN DESA, 2015b). According to UN data for the emigrant stock in 2015, 68% of emigrants went to Thailand, 14% to the United States and 5% to France. Less than 10% of emigrants passed through official channels. The outflow of workers has led to a significant increase in remittances, which reached an estimated USD 363 million, or 2% of GDP, in 2014 (OECD/CDRI, 2017; National Bank of Cambodia, 2015).

In absolute terms, the greatest movement of Cambodians is between rural areas within the country, which accounts for 51% of the total number of migrants (predominantly men) versus 28% attributed to rural-urban migration (NIS, 2008). This phenomenon, described as the "invisible flow" on account of the limited extent to which it is captured in survey data, is driven by migration from the central plains (Mekong Delta and Tonle Sap basin), where population density is highest, to forested areas in the northwest of the country near the Thai border, where it is easier for farmers to "acquire" their own land (Maltoni, 2007; Diepart, 2015).[9]

Box 1.5. **Two stages of a demographic dividend**

A demographic dividend arises from a favourable interaction of demographic and economic trends. The first phase coincides with a decline in the dependency ratio associated with falling fertility rates and thus a reduction in the number of child dependants relative to the size of the working-age population. The number of "producers" in the economy increases relative to "consumers". This dynamic can be influenced by public policies, such as interventions to reduce fertility rates. A number of Asian governments have implemented such policies, of which China's one-child policy is the most dramatic example.

To capitalise on the favourable age structure of the economy, there must be sufficient employment for the enlarged working-age population and growth in the capital stock to ensure that productivity does not decline on a per capita basis. Higher domestic savings – a corollary of the gap between production and consumption – can finance the investment required to ensure that output per worker does not fall as the size of the workforce grows.

This investment is also crucial in ensuring that the age structure of the population does not become a drag on the economy when the dependency ratio starts to increase due to population ageing. In this case, investment in both physical and human capital is essential to improve the productivity of the workforce. South Korea's investment in health services and education was an essential ingredient in its rapid transition from a low- to high-income economy (Eichengreen, Park and Shin, 2013). Policies to enhance labour force participation by women can also enhance growth rates and slow the increase in the dependency ratio (Bloom et al., 2007).

The policies implemented during the first demographic dividend have the potential to generate a second demographic dividend. As life expectancies increase, there is a strong incentive for individuals to save, which can substantially increase investment rates and thus lead to further increases in output per worker (Mason and Kinugasa, 2008). The impact of introducing public pension schemes on household savings behaviour is ambiguous, although the design of such arrangements can determine the extent to which the second demographic dividend is achieved. While unfunded or pay-as-you-go arrangements represent a direct transfer from the working-age population to retirees, funded arrangements promote asset accumulation and capital market development, which can lead to productivity gains.

Cambodia's level of urbanisation is the lowest in SEA after Lao PDR, due to the dramatic decline in urban populations resulting from the policies of the Khmer Rouge. However, it is urbanising fast. Phnom Penh was home to 1.8 million people in 2014, a larger population than all other urban areas combined. The capital was home to 16.7% of the total population in 2014, up from 8.5% in 2004 (ADB, 2014a). Urban areas across the country grew 4.1% annually between 2008 and 2013 (NIS, 2014) and the population living in all Cambodian cities is projected to continue growing, from 3.2 million in 2015 to 8.2 million in 2050 (UN DESA, 2014). As a result, the level of urbanisation will rise from 20.7% to 36.2% over the same period, far below the average urbanisation level of 64.7% projected for SEA as a whole in 2050.

Notes

1. The Cambodian Socio-Economic Survey 2014 (CSES) is the eleventh survey collecting data from household and individuals in Cambodia on different areas relating to poverty. The survey is conducted by the National Institute of Statistics (NIS) of the Ministry of Planning (MoP). The first Socio-Economic Survey was conducted in 1994. Since then, the CSES has been conducted in 1996, 1997, 1999 and 2004. Since 2007, NIS has conducted the CSES annually. The 2004 CSES was the fifth survey that was conducted and was a countrywide sample survey of villages and households. The 2004 CSES was the first survey to report income and receipts; self-evaluation of daily expenditure and consumption were reported. The monthly sample size in the 2004 CSES was 1 000 households.

   Since 2007, the Socio-Economic Survey has been conducted every year with a sample size of 300 households every month (3 600 households annually). The annual surveys are undertaken as part of the project, "Capacity Development for Socio-Economic Surveys and Planning" of the Royal Government of Cambodia. This project is supported and financed by the Swedish International Development Cooperation Agency. In 2009, the CSES was similar to the 2004 CSES, with a sample size of 1 000 households every month (12 000 households on an annual basis). See NIS (2013) for more information.

2. The Gini coefficient is a "measure of the deviation of the distribution of income among individuals or households within a country from a perfectly equal distribution. A value of 0 represents absolute equality, a value of 100 absolute inequality" (UNDP, 2013a). See *hdr.undp.org/en/content/income-gini-coefficient* (accessed 22 December 2016).

3. Note that this figure is based on a subsample of the IDPoor data. In particular, the subsample represents households included across all three waves in four provinces (Kampot, Pursat, Ratanak Kiri and Svay Rieng). Unlike other provinces, the coverage in the initial IDPoor baseline in the subsample provinces included nearly the entire rural population, thereby minimising potential bias issues. Because different regions were surveyed at different times, it is not possible to specify exact years for each wave.

4. The Law on the Protection and Promotion of the Rights of Persons with Disabilities (2009) defines individuals with a disability as "any persons who lack, lose, or damage any physical or mental functions, which result in a disturbance to their daily life or activities, such as physical, visual, hearing, intellectual impairments, mental disorders and any other types of disabilities toward the insurmountable end of the scale" (RGC, 2009). See *cambodiainvestment.gov.kh/content/uploads/2011/09/Law-on-the-Protection-and-the-Promotion-of-the-Rights-of-Persons-with-Disabilities_090812.pdf*.

5. The methodology used to derive these forecasts is described in Annex 1.A1.

6. In 2005, less than 9% of garment factories were owned by Cambodians, according to the Garment Manufacturers Association in Cambodia (USAID, 2005).
7. Peng et al. (2004) find that rice yields decline as a result of higher night-time temperatures caused by global warming.
8. Myanmar's population data is not comparable with the rest of the region but the UN calculates that its dependency ratio fell from 58.6% in 2000 to 49.7% in 2015 and will decline to 47.3% in 2050 before rising to 60.9% in 2100 (UN DESA, 2017).
9. Under the Land Law (2001), it is not legal to formally acquire forestland, which is classified as state public land, but this practice has continued on a de facto basis with the knowledge of local authorities (Diepart, 2015).

References

Adato, M. and L. Bassett (2009), "Social protection to support vulnerable children and families: The potential of cash transfers to protect education, health and nutrition", *AIDS Care*, Vol. 21, Iss. Sup. 1, Taylor & Francis, Abingdon-on-Thames, pp. 60-75, *http://dx.doi.org/10.1080/09540120903112351*.

ADB (2014), *Cambodia: Country Poverty Analysis 2014*, Asian Development Bank, Manila, *www.adb.org/documents/cambodia-country-poverty-analysis-2014*.

ADB (2013), *Gender Equality and the Labor Market: Cambodia, Kazakhstan, and the Philippines*, Asian Development Bank, Manila, *www.adb.org/sites/default/files/publication/31167/gender-equality-cambodia-philippines-kazakhstan.pdf*.

ADB and ILO (2015), *Cambodia: Addressing the Skills Gap – Employment Diagnostic Study*, Asian Development Bank and International Labour Organization, Phnom Penh, *www.adb.org/publications/cambodia-addressing-skills-gap*.

Asuyama, Y. and S. Neou (2012), "How has the Cambodian garment industry evolved?", in *Dynamics of the Garment Industry in Low-Income Countries: Experience of Asia and Africa*, Interim Report, Takahiro Fukunishi (ed.), Chousakenkyu Houkokusho, Institute of Developing Economies-Japan External Trade Organization, Chiba City, *ide.go.jp/English/Publish/Download/Report/2011/2011_410.html*.

Bloom, D.E. et al. (2007), "Fertility, female labor force participation, and the demographic dividend", *NBER Working Paper Series*, No. 13583, National Bureau of Economic Research, Cambridge, MA, *http://dx.doi.org/10.3386/w13583*.

Bullen, D. and S. Corita (2012), *Drowning in Debt: Impact of 2011 Cambodia Floods on Household Debt*, Survey Report and Findings, prepared for CARE Cambodia, Phnom Penh, *alnap.org/resource/10248*.

CARD, UNICEF and WFP (2013), *The Economic Consequences of Malnutrition in Cambodia: A Damage Assessment Report*, Council for Agricultural and Rural Development, United Nations Children's Fund and United Nations World Food Programme, Phnom Penh, *wfp.org/content/damage-assessment-report-economic-consequences-malnutrition-cambodia*.

CCCA (2012), *Cambodia Climate Change Alliance Annual Report*, Cambodia Climate Change Alliance, Phnom Penh, *kh.undp.org/content/dam/cambodia/docs/EnvEnergy/CCCAProjects/2012_Annual_Progress_Report_CCCA.pdf*.

Chang, J-H. and P. Huynh (2016), "ASEAN in transformation: The future of jobs at risk of automation", Bureau for Employers' Activities, *Working Paper* No 9, International Labour Organization, Geneva, *ilo.org/public/english/dialogue/actemp/downloads/publications/2016/asean_in_transf_2016_r2_future.pdf*.

DFID (2011), *Cash Transfers: Evidence Paper, Policy Division 2011*, Department for International Development, Government of the United Kingdom, London, webarchive, *gsdrc.org/document-library/cash-transfers-evidence-paper/*.

Diepart, J-C. (2015), "The fragmentation of land tenure systems in Cambodia: Peasants and the formalization of land rights", Country Profile No. 6: Cambodia, Agence française de développement, Paris, *orbi.ulg.ac.be/bitstream/2268/183306/1/DIEPART_2015_Fragmentation-Land-Tenure-Systems-Cambodia.pdf*.

Eichengreen, B., D. Park and K. Shin (2013), "Growth slowdowns redux: New evidence on the middle-income trap", *NBER Working Paper Series*, No. 18673, National Bureau of Economic Research, Cambridge, MA, *http://dx.doi.org/10.3386/w18673*.

Fay, M. et al. (2015), *Shock Waves: Managing the Impacts of Climate Change on Poverty*, Climate Change and Development Series, World Bank, Washington, DC, *http://dx.doi.org/10.1596/978-1-4648-0673-5*.

Francisco, H.A. et al. (2011), "Determinants of household decisions on adaptation to extreme climate events in Southeast Asia", *Research Report*, No. 2011-RR5, Economy and Environment Program for Southeast Asia Program, International Development Research Centre Regional Office for Southeast and East Asia, Singapore, *idl-bnc.idrc.ca/dspace/handle/10625/48815*.

Gallup World Poll (2016), *Gallup World Poll* (database), *gallup.com/services/170945/world-poll.aspx* (accessed March 2016).

Grantham-McGregor, S. et al. (2007), "Developmental potential in the first 5 years for children in developing countries", *The Lancet*, Vol. 369, No. 9555, Elsevier B.V., Amsterdam, pp. 60-70, *http://dx.doi.org/10.1016/S0140-6736(07)60032-4*.

Human Rights Watch (2015), "Work Faster or Get Out"*: Labour Rights Abuses in Cambodia's Garment Industry*, Human Rights Watch, New York, *features.hrw.org/features/HRW_2015_reports/Cambodia_Garment_Workers*.

IHME (2013), *Global Burden of Disease* (database), Institute for Health Metrics and Evaluation, University of Washington, Seattle, *healthdata.org/gbd/data*.

ILO (2017), "Recent trade policy developments and possible implications for Cambodia's garment and footwear sector", Cambodian Garment and Footwear Sector Bulletin, Iss. 5, International Labour Organization, Geneva, *ilo.org/asia/publications/WCMS_541288/lang--en/index.htm*.

ILO (2016), "How is Cambodia's minimum wage adjusted?", *Cambodian Garment and Footwear Sector Bulletin*, Iss. 3, International Labour Organization, Geneva, *ilo.org/asia/whatwedo/publications/WCMS_463849/lang--en/index.htm*.

ILO (2015), *Key Indicators of the Labour Market*, 9th ed., International Labour Organization, Geneva, *ilo.org/global/statistics-and-databases/research-and-databases/kilm/lang--en/index.htm*.

ILO (2013), *Global Wage Report 2012/13: Wages and Equitable Growth*, International Labour Organization, Geneva, *ilo.org/global/research/global-reports/global-wage-report/2012/WCMS_194843/lang--de/index.htm*.

ILO (2012), *Action-oriented research on gender equality and the working and living conditions of garment factory workers in Cambodia*, International Labour Organization Regional Office for Asia and the Pacific, Phnom Penh, *ilo.org/wcmsp5/groups/public/---asia/---ro-bangkok/---sro-bangkok/documents/publication/wcms_204166.pdf*.

ILO (2010), "Effects of non-contributory social transfers in developing countries: A compendium", *Working Paper*, International Labour Organization, Geneva, *research.manchester.ac.uk/portal/files/32800126/FULL_TEXT.pdf*.

ILO and NIS (2013), *Cambodia Labour Force and Child Labour Survey 2012: Child Labour Report*, International Labour Organization, International Programme on the Elimination of Child Labour and National Institute of Statistics, Phnom Penh, *ilo.org/ipecinfo/product/download.do?type=document&id=24055*.

IMF (2015), *World Economic Outlook* (database), International Monetary Fund, Washington, DC, *imf.org/external/pubs/ft/weo/2016/01/weodata/index.aspx* (accessed October 2015).

Kappel, V., A. Krauss and L. Lontzek (2010), "Over-Indebtedness and Microfinance: Constructing an Early Warning Index", responsAbility Investments for Prosperity, University of Zurich, Zurich, *cmf.uzh.ch/publications/Microfinance%20and%20OID%20-%20full%20version.pdf*.

Liv, D. (2013), *Study on the Drivers of Over-Indebtedness of Microfinance Borrowers in Cambodia: An In-depth Investigation of Saturated Areas*, Final Report, Cambodian Institute of Development Studies, Phnom Penh, *incofin.com/sites/default/files/attachments/publications/Drivers%20of%20OID-Cambodia.pdf*.

Maltoni, B. (2007), "Migration in Cambodia: Internal vs. External Flows", presented at the 8th ARPMN Conference on Migration, Development and Poverty Reduction, Fuzhou, 25-29 May 2007, International Organization for Migration, Phnom Penh, *apmrn.anu.edu.au/conferences/8thAPMRNconference/7.Maltoni.pdf*.

Martorell, R. (1995), "Results and implications of the INCAP follow-up study", *The Journal of Nutrition*. Vol. 125, No. 4, Suppl, pp. 1127S-1138S, American Society for Nutrition, Rockville, MD, *jn.nutrition.org/content/125/4_Suppl/1127S.extract*.

Mason, A. and T. Kinugasa (2008), "East Asian economic development: Two demographic dividends", *Journal of Asian Economics*, Vol. 19, No. 5-6, Elsevier B.V., Amsterdam, pp. 389-399, *http://dx.doi.org/10.1016/j.asieco.2008.09.006*.

MoEYS (2015), *Education Statistics and Indicators: 2014-2015*, Education Management Information System Office, Department of Planning, Ministry of Education, Youth and Sport, Royal Government of Cambodia, Phnom Penh, *moeys.gov.kh/en/emis/1607/1607-1607.html#.WHvhBLkzXIU*.

MoH (2007), "Community Services for the Elderly", *Country Report*, 5th Association of Southeast Asian Nations and JAPAN High Level Officials Meeting on Caring Societies, Tokyo, 27-30 August 2007, Ministry of Health, Royal Government of Cambodia, Phnom Penh, *mhlw.go.jp/bunya/kokusaigyomu/asean/asean/kokusai/siryou/dl/h19_cambodia1.pdf*.

MoP (2016), *IDPoor: Identification of Poor Households Programme* (database), Ministry of Planning, Royal Government of Cambodia, Phnom Penh, *mop.gov.kh/Projects/IDPoor/tabid/154/Default.aspx*.

National Bank of Cambodia (2015), "Cambodia Balance of Payments Statistics Bulletin – Series No. 50, Fourth Quarter 2015", National Bank of Cambodia, Royal Government of Cambodia, Phnom Penh, *nbc.org.kh/download_files/economic_research/bop_eng/BOP_Bulletin_No.50.pdf*.

NIPH, NIS and ORC Macro (2006), *Cambodia Demographic Health Survey 2005*, Final Report, National Institute of Public Health, National Institute of Statistics and Opinion Research Company [ORC] Macro, Phnom Penh, *dhsprogram.com/publications/publication-FR185-DHS-Final-Reports.cfm*.

NIS (2014), *Cambodia Socio-Economic Survey 2014*, National Institute of Statistics, Ministry of Planning, Royal Government of Cambodia, Phnom Penh.

NIS (2013), *Cambodia Socio-Economic Survey (Overview)*, National Institute of Statistics, Ministry of Planning, Royal Government of Cambodia, Phnom Penh, *nada-nis.gov.kh/index.php/catalog/19/study-description*.

NIS (2009), *Cambodia Socio-Economic Survey 2009, Household Survey 2009*, National Institute of Statistics, Ministry of Planning, Royal Government of Cambodia, Phnom Penh.

NIS (2008), *Demographic Census 2008*, Final Results, National Institute of Statistics, Ministry of Planning, Royal Government of Cambodia, Phnom Penh.

NIS (2004), *Cambodia Socio-Economic Survey 2004, Household Survey 2004*, National Institute of Statistics, Ministry of Planning, Royal Government of Cambodia, Phnom Penh.

NIS, MoH and ICF International (2015), *Cambodia Demographic Health Survey 2014*, Final Report, National Institute of Statistics and Directorate General for Health and ICF International, Phnom Penh, *dhsprogram.com/publications/publication-fr312-dhs-final-reports.cfm*.

NIS, MoH and ICF Macro (2011), *Cambodia Demographic Health Survey 2010*, Final Report, National Institute of Statistics, Directorate for Health and ICF Macro, Phnom Penh, *dhsprogram.com/publications/publication-FR249-DHS-Final-Reports.cfm*.

OECD (2017), *Interrelations between Public Policies, Migration and Development*, OECD Publishing, Paris, *http://dx.doi.org/10.1787/9789264265615-en*.

OECD/CDRI (2017), *Interrelations between Public Policies, Migration and Development in Cambodia*, OECD Publishing, Paris, *http://dx.doi.org/10.1787/9789264273634-en*.

Ovesen, J., I.B. Trankell and J. Öjendal (1996), *When Every Household is an Island: Social Organization and Power Structures in Rural Cambodia*, Uppsala Research Reports in Cultural Anthropology, No. 15, Department of Cultural Anthropology, Uppsala University and Swedish International Development Cooperation Agency, Stockholm, *uu.diva-portal.org/smash/record.jsf?pid=diva2%3A71286&dswid=-3557*.

Peng, S. et al. (2004), "Rice yields decline with higher night temperature from global warming", *Proceedings of the National Academy of Sciences of the United States of America*, Vol. 101, No. 27, United States National Academy of Sciences, Washington, DC, pp. 9971-9975, *http://dx.doi.org/10.1073/pnas.0403720101*.

Pollitt, E. et al. (1995), "Nutrition in Early Life and the Fulfillment of Intellectual Potential", *Journal of Nutrition*, Vol. 125, No. 4, Suppl., American Society for Nutrition, Rockville, MD, pp. 1111S-1118S, *jn.nutrition.org/content/125/4_Suppl/1111S.extract*.

RGC (2013), "Cambodia Climate Change Strategic Plan 2014-2023", National Climate Change Committee, Royal Government of Cambodia, Phnom Penh, *bb.undp.org/content/dam/cambodia/docs/EnvEnergy/CCCAProjects/Cambodia%20climate%20change%20strategic%20plan%202014-2023.pdf*.

RGC (2009), "Law on the Protection and the Promotion of the Rights of Persons with Disabilities, Royal Government of Cambodia", Phnom Penh, *cambodiainvestment.gov.kh/content/uploads/2011/09/Law-on-the-Protection-and-the-Promotion-of-the-Rights-of-Persons-with-Disabilities_090812.pdf*.

RGC (1997), "Kram (Law) Dated March 13, 1997 on the Labour Law", Royal Government of Cambodia, Phnom Penh, *ilo.org/dyn/travail/docs/701/Labour%20Law.pdf*.

Tong, K. (2012), "Analysing chronic poverty in rural Cambodia: Evidence from panel data", *CDRI Working Paper Series*, No. 66, Cambodia Development Resource Institute, Phnom Penh. *citeseerx.ist.psu.edu/viewdoc/download?doi=10.1.1.920.6917&rep=rep1&type=pdf*.

UN DESA (2017), *World Population Prospects: The 2017 Revision*, United Nations Department of Economic and Social Affairs, New York, *un.org/en/development/desa/population/publications*.

UN DESA (2015a), *World Population Prospects: The 2015 Revision*, United Nations Department of Economic and Social Affairs, New York, *un.org/en/development/desa/population/publications*.

UN DESA (2015b), *Trends in International Migrant Stock: The 2015 Revision*, United Nations Department of Economic and Social Affairs, New York, *un.org/en/development/desa/population/migration/data/estimates2/estimates15.shtml*.

UN DESA (2014), *World Urbanization Prospects: The 2014 Revision*, United Nations Department of Economic and Social Affairs, New York.

UNDP (2016), *Shaping the Future: How Changing Demographics Can Power Human Development*, Asia-Pacific Human Development Report, United Nations Development Programme, New York, *hdr.undp.org/sites/default/files/rhdr2016-full-report-final-version1.pdf*.

UNDP (2015), *Human Development Report 2015: Work for Human Development*, United Nations Development Programme, New York, *hdr.undp.org/en/2015-report*.

UNDP (2014), "Competitiveness and linkages in Cambodia's manufacturing sector", *Discussion Paper*, No. 12, United Nations Development Programme, New York, *kh.undp.org/content/cambodia/en/home/library/poverty/competitiveness-and-linkages-in-cambodias-manufacturing-sector.html*.

UNDP (2013a), "Income Gini coefficient", webpage, United Nations Development Programme, New York, *hdr.undp.org/en/content/income-gini-coefficient* (accessed 22 December 2016).

UNDP (2013b), *Microinsurance Study: The Understanding and Needs of Low-Income Populations regarding* Microinsurance, United Nations Development Programme Cambodia, Phnom Penh, *kh.undp.org/content/cambodia/en/home/library/poverty/microinsurance-study.html*.

UNESCO (2016), *UNESCO Institute of Statistics* (database), United Nations Educational, United Nations Scientific and Cultural Organization Institute of Statistics, Montreal, *uis.unesco.org* (accessed July 2016).

UNICEF (2015), *UNICEF Data: Monitoring the Situation of Children and Women* (database), United Nations Children's Fund, New York, *data.unicef.org/resources* (accessed July 2016).

USAID (2011), *Dropout Trend Analysis: Cambodia*, Dropout School Prevention Pilot Program, United States Agency for International Development, Washington, DC, *schooldropoutprevention.com/wp-content/files/reports/Trend_Analysis_Cambodia_English.pdf*.

USAID (2005), *Measuring Competitiveness and Labor Productivity in Cambodia's Garment Industry*, Trade Capacity Building (TCB) Project, United States Agency for International Development, Washington, DC, *pdf.usaid.gov/pdf_docs/Pnade137.pdf*.

von Grebmer, K. et al. (2015), *Global Hunger Index : Armed conflict and the challenge of hunger*, International Food Policy Research Institute, Concern Worldwide, Welthungerhilfe, World Peace Foundation/Tufts University, Bonn, *ifpri.org/publication/2015-global-hunger-index-armed-conflict-and-challenge-hunger*.

WFP (forthcoming), *Using Social Protection Instruments to Foster Food and Nutrition Security: Draft Mission Report Cambodia*, United Nations World Food Programme, Rome.

World Bank (2016), *World Development Indicators* (database), World Bank, Washington, DC, *data.worldbank.org/products/wdi* (accessed April 2016).

World Bank (2015a), *World Development Indicators* (database), World Bank, Washington, DC, *data.worldbank.org/products/wdi*.

World Bank (2015b), *Cambodian Agriculture in Transition: Opportunities and Risks*, Economic and Sector Work, Report No. 96308-KH, International Bank for Reconstruction and Development and World Bank, Washington, DC, *worldbank.org/en/news/feature/2015/08/19/cambodian-agriculture-in-transition-opportunities-and-risks*.

World Bank (2015c), "Maintaining high growth", *Cambodia Economic Update Working Paper*, April 2015, World Bank, Phnom Penh, *openknowledge.worldbank.org/handle/10986/21904*.

World Bank (2014a), *Where Have All the Poor Gone? Cambodia Poverty Assessment 2013*, World Bank, Washington, DC, *documents.worldbank.org/curated/en/824341468017405577/pdf/ACS45450REVISE00English0260May02014.pdf*.

World Bank (2014b), "Cambodian agriculture in transition: Opportunities and risks", Feature Story, 15 August 2015, World Bank, Washington, DC, *worldbank.org/en/news/feature/2015/08/19/cambodian-agriculture-in-transition-opportunities-and-risks*.

ANNEX 1.A1

Methodology for the Social Protection System Review

The Social Protection System Review (SPSR) for Cambodia is the first application of the SPSR tool. The SPSR is an analytical tool that has been designed by the European Union Social Protection Systems Programme (EU-SPS) to support developing countries that are in the process of establishing or expanding a social protection system. The SPSR takes a holistic view of a country's social protection system, examining its three pillars – social assistance (including social health protection), social insurance and labour market programmes – within the country's broader policy context. The review examines questions of policy coherence within the social protection sector, as well as with other relevant policy areas.

The SPSR takes a forward-looking approach, providing not only a diagnostic of the current state of a country's social protection system but also highlighting future challenges and policy options for addressing them. The tool examines the country's demographics, poverty dynamics, labour market trends and public finance system in so far as these have implications for social protection. It also analyses how social protection expenditure is financed and its financial sustainability over the long term.

The SPSR examines the extent to which a social protection system provides effective and equitable coverage for the poor and those who are vulnerable to poverty. It analyses how far the system contributes to reducing poverty, vulnerability and inequality as well as examining the extent to which it has fostered more inclusive growth, defined as an improvement of living standards and the sharing of the benefits of increased prosperity evenly across social groups. The analysis will include non-monetary dimensions that matter for well-being, such as broader measures of deprivation, employment prospects, health outcomes, educational opportunities or vulnerability to adverse environmental factors.

Methodology

The SPSR is conducted in close collaboration with the government, development partners and local research institutes. Data on social protection coverage and related information is gathered as far as possible from official sources, including administrative data and household surveys. Key informant interviews with social protection stakeholders are also an integral part of the application of the SPSR.

The SPSR examines five dimensions of a country's social protection system:

- Need
- Coverage
- Effectiveness
- Sustainability
- Coherence

Need

The first component of the SPSR conducts forward-looking needs analysis to identify demand for social protection today and to forecast how demand is likely to change in the future. This analysis establishes a vulnerability profile by providing a diagnostic of poverty, multi-dimensional risks and vulnerabilities. Innovative techniques are applied to understand the dynamics and determinants of poverty and vulnerability, while harmonised and comparable indicators are used to benchmark across countries. New or emerging risks are included in this vulnerability profile, including economic, demographic or environmental trends.

Coverage

This component of the SPSR examines the extent to which the existing social protection system covers the needs identified by the first component through a threefold approach. First, it provides an overview of social protection provision that examines the legal and policy framework, institutions with a social protection mandate, and social protection programmes themselves. Second, it provides an overview of the system's characteristics in terms of high-level indicators as available through national data and international databases for benchmarking. Finally, it identifies gaps or mismatches between existing social protection schemes vis-à-vis the previously identified risks.

Effectiveness

The SPSR assesses the effectiveness of a country's social protection system according to the adequacy, efficiency, and equity of the key programmes identified by the coverage component. Through detailed analysis of these effectiveness dimensions, the SPSR determines the extent to which the programmes and the social protection system as a whole alleviate poverty, reduce inequality and address risks and vulnerabilities.

Sustainability

This component of the SPSR assesses the financial sustainability of the existing social protection system and explores whether fiscal space exists to expand it according to the recommendations that might emerge from the SPSR. An important objective is to maximise the potential of the fiscal system to achieve the goals of social protection by aligning the design of different financing mechanisms to the goals of the social protection strategy.

Coherence

Coherence analysis examines the extent to which the instruments, institutions and processes that comprise the social protection system are aligned and integrated. It also analyses the interactions between social protection and other aspects of government. In so doing, it demonstrates the extent to which a systematic approach exists and the feasibility of establishing or enhancing such an approach in the future.

Output

Taken together, these five dimensions provide a diagnostic of a country's social protection system. This analysis forms the basis of recommendations to support the development the social protection system that are developed in partnership with the country itself to ensure relevance and applicability. Both the diagnostic and the recommendations form part of the SPSR, which is published jointly with the government.

Country-specific application

The SPSR is tailored to the context of each country where it is applied. As a result, the extent to which different components are analysed varies according to a number of factors, including a country's definition of social protection, the level of development of existing social protection provision, the priorities of the government and the availability of data. The SPSR also takes into account other analytical work carried out by the government or development partners, with a view to avoiding duplication of effort or contradictory results and recommendations.

The application of the SPSR relies on close consultation with government ministries and other relevant stakeholders to ensure the output reflects the needs and priorities of the social protection sector. Throughout the process, a close dialogue is maintained with government counterparts and, if requested and feasible, the analysis can be conducted jointly with government staff and/ or local researchers.

The SPSR in Cambodia

The SPSR for Cambodia was carried out over a period of 18 months, between February 2016 and August 2017. The counterpart for the SPSR within the Cambodian government was the Council for Agricultural and Rural Development (CARD), though the exercise was also carried out in close collaboration with the Ministry of Economy and Finance (MoEF). Numerous missions were undertaken to Cambodia over this period and a policy workshop was held in June 2016 to discuss the diagnostic analysis and identify priorities for the SPSR. This workshop was attended by policy makers, development partners and representatives of civil society.

ANNEX 1.A2

Methodology for calculating long-term population growth and productivity

The calculations for the structure of output and employment in 2050 are based on an assumed rate of growth in labour productivity combined with United Nations projections for the size of the population and the level of urbanisation.

The model assumes that output per worker will grow at a constant rate of 4.5% per annum between 2020 and 2050. With growth in the working population expected to average 1.1% over this period, this would produce a rate of GDP growth between 2020 and 2050 of 5.6% per annum (assuming the productivity of capital remains constant) while per capita incomes will rise by 4.7% per annum. The rate of growth will decelerate after 2030 as the growth rate of the working-age population slows. This projection is less optimistic than the World Bank's long-term projection for the period 2015-2050, which forecasts average annual GDP growth of 6.9% (World Bank, 2015c).

To project how the structure of output is likely to change between 2020 and 2050, the model identifies productivity rates for the agricultural sector and for industry and services combined. The increase in output per worker in agriculture is assumed at 3% per annum, somewhat faster than the 2.4% between 2000 and 2014. The rate of increase in the rural population between 2015 and 2050 is projected at 0.4% per annum, and this will be assumed to be the rate of growth of agricultural employment, so the rate of increase in agricultural output is 3.4% per annum. This in turn implies a rise in industrial and services output of 6.3%. The difference between these respective growth rates generates the long-term changes in the structure of output identified in the text.

Chapter 2

A social protection system under construction

This chapter examines the adequacy of social protection in Cambodia in light of the risks and vulnerabilities identified in Chapter 1. Social protection in Cambodia is well established in legal and policy frameworks, including the Social Protection Policy Framework approved in 2017. While Cambodia has a variety of social assistance, social health protection, social insurance and labour market programmes in place, coverage is low and provision is highly fragmented. The current capacity of social protection to reduce poverty and vulnerability is therefore limited.

Health Equity Funds are emerging as an exception to this situation. These provide relatively high levels of coverage among the poor population and are growing rapidly, thus providing a potential avenue towards universal health coverage.

As Chapter 1 explains, monetary poverty has fallen sharply in Cambodia since the early 2000s. The proportion of poor individuals fell from 63% to 13% between 2004 and 2014 while human development indicators have also shown strong improvement, though there remains considerable scope for further gains. These achievements were largely attributed to the rapid growth of the garment and footwear sector, strong agricultural growth and favourable demographics. Yet despite these improvements, the majority of the population remains poor or vulnerable. Moreover, a number of trends threaten to undo much of the gains achieved in recent years. To what extent are Cambodia's social protection instruments able to address these current and future livelihood challenges?

This chapter examines the adequacy of social protection in Cambodia in light of the risks and vulnerabilities identified in Chapter 1. Adequacy is assessed by looking at both selected supply-side indicators (such the existence of social protection legal frameworks, instruments and programmes; the overall amount allocated to public social protection spending; benefit levels) and demand-side indicators, such as coverage. Particular attention is paid to the extent to which various elements of the social protection system are appropriate for the challenges facing Cambodia and the extent to which they are coherent with each other.

The legal and strategic frameworks for social protection are under development

Informal social protection networks have a long history of alleviating poverty and protecting vulnerable groups in Cambodia, and they continue to play an important role today (RGC, 2011a). However, the upheavals in Cambodian society over the past 50 years – not only protracted periods of conflict but also the process of economic development – have disrupted these networks, even at the family level. As a consequence, a clear role for public intervention has emerged.

The alleviation of poverty and support for vulnerable groups have featured prominently in Cambodia's development plans since 1993, and a range of social protection instruments have been implemented over this period. Poverty alleviation was a cornerstone of the National Program to Rehabilitate and Develop Cambodia (1994), which recognised that rural areas were especially vulnerable and underdeveloped following the events of the previous two decades.

The First Socio-Economic Development Plan (SEDP) (1996-2000) was not only a critical moment in Cambodia's economic development, promoting its orientation to a market economy and the advancement of the garment sector, but it also established clear priorities in terms of job creation, poverty alleviation and social reconstruction. These priorities were maintained by the Second SEDP (2001-2005), which identified economic and social development as one of three pillars of its triangular strategy, and by the National Strategic Development Plan (NSDP) (2006-2010). The term "social protection" featured in the Poverty Reduction Strategy Paper (2002) and was integrated into the update to the NSDP (2008-2012), during which period the National Social Protection Strategy for the Poor and Vulnerable (NSPS) was approved.

In 2017, the Royal Government of Cambodia (RGC) published a Social Protection Policy Framework (SPPF), which lays the foundation for an integrated social protection system. The main goal of the SPPF, which covers the period from 2016 to 2025, is to harmonise and strengthen existing schemes to increase the effectiveness, transparency, consistency and coverage of the entire social protection system (RGC, 2016). The SPPF is the first policy document of its kind in Cambodia to cover social assistance, social insurance and social health protection, thus providing the basis for the systematisation of various schemes and initiatives. The development of the SPPF was led by the Ministry of Economy and Finance (MoEF) in close collaboration with various line ministries and the Council for Agricultural and Rural Development (CARD).

The SPPF defines six main goals: i) implement a new social assistance programme to expand the coverage of current schemes; ii) expand social security to achieve universal coverage for health and pensions; iii) review and update the institutional arrangements to establish a National Social Protection Council; iv) improve the investment environment for social protection; v) integrate identification and registration systems; and vi) promote citizen understanding of social protection.

The SPPF will look to realise the right to social protection enshrined in Cambodia's Constitution. Article 36 of the Constitution, which was promulgated in 1993, entitles every Khmer citizen to obtain social security and other benefits determined by law. Article 75 commits the state to establishing a social security system for workers and employees. The Constitution recognises specific vulnerable groups, requiring the state to provide support to mothers, children, people with disabilities and families of deceased soldiers. It also commits the state to supporting women, especially those in rural areas, to access employment and medical care, send their children to school and enjoy decent living conditions.

The Labour Law (1997), the Insurance Law (2000) and the Law on Social Security Schemes for Persons Defined by the Provisions of the Labour Law (2002) established the legislative foundation for the rights of workers, including access to social security. High levels of informality and low levels of monitoring have constrained the implementation and enforcement of this legislation. The rights of women and children have been partially addressed through the Law on the Prevention of Domestic Violence and the Protection of Victims (2005) and the Law on Suppression of Human Trafficking and Sexual Exploitation (2007), although this legislation stops short of the entitlements articulated by the Constitution. Meanwhile, a rights-based approach to social protection is evident in the Law on the Protection and Promotion of the Rights of People with Disabilities (2009).

Various policy action plans and decrees provide a framework for social protection. A National Policy for the Elderly was established in 2003, which identifies the extent of the RGC's responsibilities for supporting the elderly and is currently being updated, while a National Policy for Early Childhood Care and Development was endorsed in 2010. The Labour Law (1997) and Prakas (ministerial decree) No. 106 on the Prohibition of Hazardous Child Labour (2004) identify the kinds of work that are permissible for children at different ages. In 2014, the Ministry of Women's Affairs (MoWA) published a five-year strategic plan for gender equality and women's empowerment.

In 2014, the Ministry of Labour and Vocational Training (MoLVT) adopted the Social Protection Strategy for Persons Defined by the Provisions of the Labour Law Year: 2014-2018. Successive strategic plans for health and education have also articulated the rights of poor and vulnerable individuals to access services.

CARD acts as a co-ordinating body for social protection for the RGC, in particular for social assistance programmes (CARD, 2010). It co-ordinates line ministries and development partners in the framework of the NSPS. As such, it co-ordinates a variety of programmes, including school feeding programmes and scholarships implemented by the Ministry of Education, Youth and Sport (MoEYS); technical vocational education and training (TVET) at the MoLVT; various allowances managed by the Ministry of Social Affairs, Veterans and Youth Rehabilitation (MoSVY); and health services provided by the Ministry of Health (MoH).

Social assistance is limited in scope and coverage

Cambodia's largest social assistance programmes are focused on human development and emergency response. Smaller programmes exist for other vulnerable groups but funding levels are very low. Social assistance programmes receive substantial donor assistance but the RGC is gradually scaling up and assuming financial responsibility. Annex 2.A1 provides a detailed inventory.

Human development

Programmes to support the development of Cambodia's children are at the centre of its social assistance provision. School scholarships, implemented by the RGC and donors, are well established. There are run on an unconditional basis but the programmes are only implemented in certain regions, to children in certain grades.

Since 2011, the MoEYS and the World Food Programme (WFP) have implemented different scholarship programmes in selected regions. The programme provides benefits worth USD 60 per year for children in grades 4 to 10 (or aged 9 to 15) from poor households (as identified by the IDPoor targeting mechanism).

The RGC's new SPPF places a high priority on scaling up scholarship programmes. Among other goals, the framework would expand them to more geographical areas, include all grades (1 to 3 and up to grade 12), increase the monthly allowance and gradually expand government financing of these schemes.

An evaluation of CESSP Scholarship Programme showed school enrolment to be very responsive to even modest incentives provided to households, with an observed increase in school enrolment and attendance of approximately 25% (Filmer and Schady, 2009). There was no significant incremental impact on the enrolment rate between receiving an annual grant of USD 45 or USD 60, highlighting the importance of rigorous impact evaluations to inform key design choices, such as benefit levels.

School feeding programmes also exist. As of 2016, school feeding programmes include: i) school meals programmes funded by development partners, primarily the WFP; ii) school meal programmes supported by the RGC; iii) take-home ration programmes; and iv) home-grown meal programmes. Currently, donors fund most of these schemes. However, the RGC plans to take over funding responsibility gradually and expand the programmes to more areas.

The MoH implements a maternal and child health and nutrition scheme. The scheme pays cash transfers to poor mothers and their children aged under two as a means of improving nutrition levels and cognitive and physical development of children, especially during the first 1 000 days of life (from conception) (MoH, 2008). It comprises three pilot projects:

- A programme funded by the World Bank and implemented by the Secretariat of the National Committee for Sub-National Democratic Development (NCDDS) (which ended in 2016);
- A programme funded by the United Nations Children's Fund (UNICEF) and implemented by CARD; and
- A programme funded by Save the Children and implemented by district and commune-level authorities.

The SPPF outlines plans to continue and expand schemes related to maternal and child health and nutrition, with several options considered going forward.

Emergency response

The Emergency Food Assistance Project (EFAP) was established in 2008 to alleviate the food insecurity of 500 000 poor and vulnerable individuals following sharp increases in global commodity prices. The higher prices helped to reduce poverty among Cambodian farmers who were net producers of crops but the negative impact on net consumers of crops was severe. The scheme is majority funded by grants and loans by development partners, including the Asian Development Bank (ADB), WFP and Global Agriculture and Food Security Program. The RGC also contributes to the financing of EFAP, which is managed through the MoEF.

The EFAP is now coming to an end. Originally planned for 2010-14, the RGC extended and expanded the project to include other programmes, such as the cash-for-work (CfW) and food-for-work (FfW) programmes and scholarship programmes targeting poor households. The RGC has sought to institutionalise the programme through the establishment of the Cambodia Food Reserve System (FRS), which was established in 2012. The MoEF will manage the scheme while the National Committee for Disaster Management (NCDM) will co-ordinate its implementation nationwide.

The RGC makes emergency relief funds available on an ad hoc basis but relies heavily on humanitarian aid. The MoSVY receives an annual budget allocation to support initiatives assisting victims of natural disasters and other vulnerable groups. However, it remains heavily reliant on external emergency relief in the event of a natural disaster.[1] The support provided by donor partners is not solely financial; an NCDM directive of 2010 integrates the Red Cross of Cambodia into the RGC's emergency response plans at the local level (RGC, 2014).

In 2015, the RGC launched a programme called Reducing the Vulnerability of Cambodian Rural Livelihoods through Enhanced Sub-national Climate Change Planning and Execution of Priority Actions. This initiative aims to reduce the vulnerability of rural Cambodians, especially land-poor and/or female-headed households, through investments in small-scale water management infrastructure, technical assistance to resilient agricultural practices, and capacity-building support for improved food production in home gardens. This four-year programme started in 2015 and is being implemented by the Ministry of Environment (MoE) and the NCDD-S, with support from the United Nations Development Programme (UNDP), in ten districts of Siem Reap and Kampong Thom.

Vulnerable groups

Public care facilities – a last resort for the most vulnerable children – are being scaled back. Some 11 788 children under the age of 18 (including orphans, as well as child victims of trafficking or sexual exploitation) lived in residential care across the country in 2015 (UNICEF, 2016). Local authorities play an important role in targeting and referring these children to residential care facilities. However, these institutions operate in an under-regulated and poorly monitored environment, often to the detriment of vulnerable children (UNICEF, 2011).

The RGC favours family- and community-based care and considers residential care a last resort for orphaned or abandoned children. In accordance with the Alternative Care Policy, the RGC plans to reduce by 30% the overall number (both public and private) of residential care facilities by 2018, at the same time strengthening home-based care systems to reduce demand for these types of facilities. This transition in the care model requires that a mature foster care system be in place; the absence of this raises concerns for the situation of vulnerable children in the interim period.

A social pension does not exist in Cambodia at present. However, the elderly receive support through associations that bring the elderly in small communities together, providing various services, such as health training and home visits, work opportunities, social activities and training in accessing benefits (HelpAge International, 2010). The cost of this programme is minimal. As indicated in the new SPPF, the RGC is considering cash transfers as an elderly allowance to complement and support better access to health care services and to partly subsidise basic daily expenses.

The RGC established a disability allowance in 2013 with a total budget of USD 1 million. The programme is intended to provide a monthly allowance of USD 5 to individuals with disabilities who are poor, elderly or without family support. However, there have been significant challenges in disbursing this fund.

Coverage

Social assistance coverage is extremely low. Despite limited official data on social assistance programmes, it is possible to make conservative estimates of coverage rates for certain programmes based on the Cambodia Socio-Economic Survey (CSES). However, important discrepancies exist between administrative data and coverage rates from household surveys: administrative data for 2014 indicated a scholarship coverage rate of 5% for school-age children, while the 2014 CSES indicated that about 2.3% of households with at least one child attending school received a scholarship, either from the RGC or from non-governmental organisations (NGOs).

The low coverage is partly by design. A large majority of social assistance programmes – whether funded by the RGC or donors – are means tested and employ the Identification of Poor Households Programme (IDPoor) system to target poor households (Box 2.1). Social assistance also has a heavy rural bias: most of the programmes are aimed principally at rural areas and, as a result, the IDPoor system is mostly applied in rural areas as well.

However, the low social assistance coverage also reflects the fact that, as noted above, the sector comprises a number of small, uncoordinated schemes (or pilot schemes) with different implementers and different sources of finance. A single, nationwide cash transfer does not exist for any group.

Box 2.1. **IDPoor is enhancing poverty reduction through better identification**

The IDPoor Programme was established in 2011 as an integral part of the RGC's efforts to reduce poverty through better identification. Sub-Decree No. 291 on the Identification of Poor Households tasks the Ministry of Planning (MoP) with co-ordinating and monitoring the identification of poor households.[2] The decree also commits the MoP to providing technical guidance to relevant government institutions, non-governmental organisations and local communities taking part in the identification of poor households, as well as collecting, analysing and disseminating data. According to the sub-decree, the procedures and methodologies for IDPoor differ for rural and urban areas, although the IDPoor programme has until recently overwhelmingly targeted rural populations.

The process of identifying poor households places great emphasis on transparency. The IDPoor Programme is implemented according to a well-developed procedure, from the MoP through to the village level (see Annex 2.A2 for rural IDPoor indicators and procedure). A group of village representatives score and categorise households as poor, very poor or non-poor. "Poverty" is not defined in terms of income but according to broader measures of deprivation, which is appropriate given that multi-dimensional poverty is more prevalent than monetary poverty, as discussed in Chapter 1 (NIS, MoH and ICF International, 2015; NIS, 2014).

Households categorised as "poor and living below the food poverty line" (corresponding to an IDPoor 2 level) or as "poor and living above the food poverty line" (IDPoor 1 level) receive an Equity Access Card, which enables them to access a variety of programmes and services. The household can provide feedback during a consultative village meeting and file a grievance with the Commune Council if unsatisfied with the updated categorisation, a built-in process that makes the IDPoor database a corroborative, transparent and granular register, although no official statistics have published at this time regarding the success of grievance procedures.

In 2015, the RGC conducted the first field test of the questionnaire for urban areas in Phnom Penh, Khan Tuol Kork and Sangkat Boeung Saland. Data collection for the first round of urban IDPoor is currently on-going. Both the rural and urban IDPoor questionnaires include income and asset variables to determine household poverty levels. The urban questionnaire, however, adds specific criteria, namely illness, injury, disability, education and debt. Relative to other vulnerability factors, it gives severe illness and disability high importance in the scoring system (up to 15% of the total score, compared with up to 6% for lack of education/children not attending school, and up to 4.5% for household debt). The urban IDPoor Programme will include activities to increase awareness and participation (Deutsche Gesellschaft für Internationale Zusammenarbeit [GIZ], 2016).[3]

Box 2.1. **IDPoor is enhancing poverty reduction through better identification** *(cont.)*

The IDPoor Programme identified approximately 20% of the Cambodian population as poor (NIS, 2014). Figure 2.1 illustrates the distribution of IDPoor cardholders by consumption decile according to the 2014 CSES. Less than half of IDPoor cardholders are classified as poor using the national definition (per capita consumption under poverty line of KHR 149 524 in real 2009 prices in 2014), while more than half of those targeted by IDPoor fall under the national non-poor but vulnerable definition (1.5 times the national poverty line).

The cost of implementing IDPoor, including the identification and enrolment of poor individuals, was estimated at USD 581 per village or USD 2.8 per individual in 2012 (Chantum, 2012). See Annex 2.A2 for village-level rural IDPoor indicators and procedure.

Figure 2.1. **The IDPoor system is effective at targeting the poor**

Distribution of IDPoor beneficiaries by consumption decile, 2014

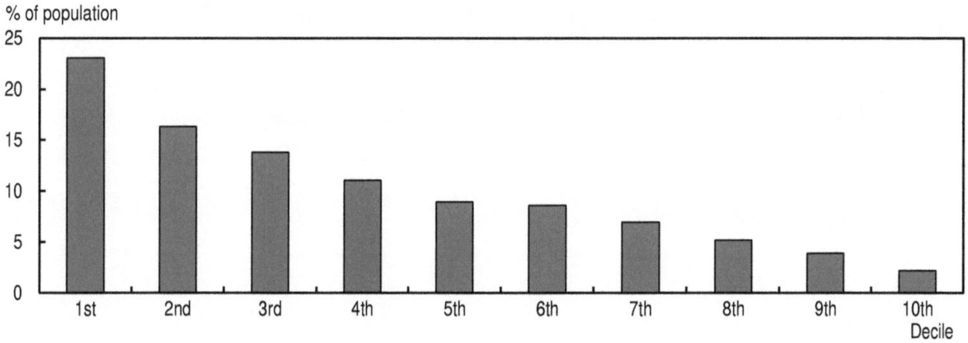

Note: The deciles of household consumption per capita in 2014 Cambodian riel (KHR) are defined according to the following cut-offs: 131 675 / 157 611 / 181 599 / 203 509 / 228 697 / 258 686 / 294 930 / 352 555 / 456 316.
Source: Authors' calculations based on NIS (2014), *Cambodia Socio-Economic Survey 2014*, available at *nada-nis.gov.kh/index.php/catalog/CSES*.

Approximately 90% of those targeted by IDPoor are classified as poor or vulnerable by CSES data and national thresholds. Assuming a similar distribution between beneficiaries and benefits of the IDPoor cardholders, the targeting performance is on par with that of conditional cash transfers in Jamaica and Paraguay and performs slightly better than Colombia's Familias en Acción programme (World Bank, 2015). However, since Cambodia's number of poor and vulnerable stands at approximately 7.3 million people, compared with IDPoor's coverage of 3 million, the programme excludes significant numbers of poor and vulnerable individuals.

The expansion of IDPoor to cover urban areas would significantly improve the situation for the households living in poverty in urban areas by integrating them into the social protection system.

Social health protection is at the forefront of social protection

Universal health coverage (UHC) is an explicit goal of the SPPF. In order to achieve this, the RGC intends to consolidate and expand the Health Equity Funds (HEF) and to enrol formal sector workers in social health insurance, which has recently been rolled out at scale.

Active since 2000 and expanded to all referral hospitals and most health centres in 2015, HEF have significantly improved access to health care services for poor and vulnerable households and lowered out-of-pocket health expenditure (Bigdeli and Annear, 2009; Ensor et al., 2017). A study looking at a subset of districts concluded that HEF have reduced out-of-pocket expenditure for health by 35% on average and by 42% for the bottom two quintiles of the income distribution (Flores et al., 2013).

HEF are non-contributory arrangements that are financed partly by the RGC and partly by donors. HEF directly reimburse to the relevant facility the costs associated with service uptake, including direct health care services and prescribed medication. They also cover costs associated with accessing these services (such as transportation and caregiver support). The HEF operational model has undergone some developments in recent years, notably regarding its promotion and verification elements.

HEF are targeted at poor individuals through either a pre-identification or a post-identification mechanism. In the case of pre-identification, households identified as poor by the IDPoor database (Box 2.1) receive an Equity Access Card, which qualifies them for free health care. HEF cover approximately 2.9 million people who hold IDPoor Equity Access Cards, representing just under 20% of the population (Annear et al., 2016). In the post-identification process, health care facilities identify patients that seek treatment as "very poor", "poor" (both eligible for fee exemption) or "non-poor" (not eligible) using a simplified form provided by the MoH. Each post-identified individual receives a Priority Access Card, which is valid for a period of one year.

The post-identification mechanism can limit errors of exclusion from the system. However, by mostly targeting the IDPoor Equity Access cardholders, the programme risks excluding other vulnerable groups, including individuals with chronic diseases or terminal illnesses, those near poverty (many of whom work in hazardous environments) and the urban poor. As a result, a large proportion of Cambodians are at risk of falling into poverty when they suffer a health shock because they are forced to rely on out-of-pocket payments to finance their treatment.

Even for those covered by HEF, non-financial barriers remain. Only 26% of HEF beneficiaries sought health care in the public sector, meaning that they instead rely on (potentially expensive) treatment in the private sector. Also, those covered by HEF had only 0.54 visits to health centres per year compared to 0.66 in the total population (Annear et al., 2016). This tendency is likely to reflect various factors, including physical or socio-economic barriers to accessing public health services as well as concerns about the quality of medical services in facilities covered by HEF and awareness of entitlements among beneficiaries (Fernandes Antunes and Jacobs, 2016).

Other social health protection measures in Cambodia include a user-fee exemption policy and Community Based Health Insurance (CBHI) schemes. The nationwide user-fee exemption policy for poor households has been only partially implemented because of budget constraints and gaps in modalities for channelling waiver reimbursements to facilities (ILO, 2012; WHO, 2015).

CBHI schemes, meanwhile, have been operational in Cambodia since 1999. They cover members' user fees for access to primary health care at contracted public health centres. CBHI coverage has stagnated at less than 1% of the population and their role has declined in recent years (Bigdeli et al., 2016). Adverse selection[4] in enrolment, low capacity to contribute and a resultant lack of risk pooling are recognised globally as constraints to expansion of CBHI-type mechanisms (Mathaeur et al., 2017).

As of 2012, the number of people included under any social health protection scheme in Cambodia was second-lowest in Southeast Asia (Figure 2.2) after Lao PDR (Van Minh et al., 2014). Thailand has achieved near full population coverage in recent years thanks in part to its Universal Coverage scheme, which covers the poorest 60% of the population, while Malaysia's high population coverage is ensured by a universal entitlement to free or near-free care at the point of service in public health facilities.

It is important to note that population coverage is just one dimension of UHC (WHO, 2010). The concept also includes service coverage (the range and quality of services that are provided) and financial coverage (the level of out-of-pocket payments for individuals who are covered).

Figure 2.2. **Health insurance coverage is low by regional standards**

Coverage of health insurance in SEA (2012)

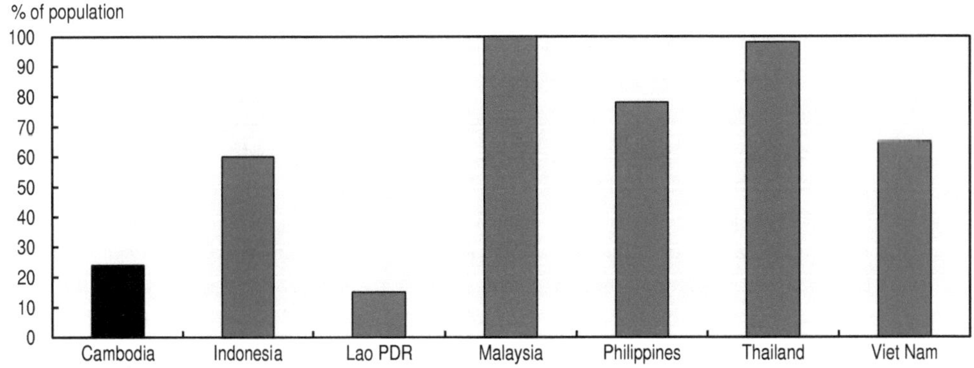

Source: Van Minh, H. et al. (2014), "Progress toward universal health coverage in ASEAN", available at *http://dx.doi.org/10.3402/gha.v7.25856*.

Large gaps exist in social insurance coverage

Cambodia's social insurance arrangements are poorly developed, even for formal-sector employees. The right to social security is enshrined in the Constitution and the Labour Law (1997) yet workers in the formal sector only have access to a limited range of instruments. However, there are signs that this situation is changing.

At present, the civil service and the military are entitled to statutory pension arrangements but do not have access to health insurance, while formal-sector workers have access to health insurance and employment-injury arrangements but lack a statutory pension arrangement. Workers in the informal sector, who typically endure more vulnerable working conditions, do not have access to social insurance.

Pensions for retirement, death and disability

Cambodia's only statutory pension arrangements are for civil servants and the military: the National Social Security Fund for Civil Servants (NSSF-C) and the National Fund for Veterans (NFV). These arrangements were established in 2008 and 2010 respectively to formalise social insurance coverage for state employees.[5] The NSSF-C covers current and retired civil servants while the NFV provides social security benefits and entitlements to military veterans and current armed forces personnel. Both schemes provide benefits in the event of retirement, death or disability to workers or their dependants (see Annex 2.A1 for benefit details) (MoEF, forthcoming).

As of 2016, the schemes covered an estimated 180 000 civil servants and 87 500 police and armed forces staff. To date, the fiscus finances all benefits paid by the NSSF-C and NFV. A Prakas issued in 2008 specified contribution rates for the NSSF-C, requiring pension contributions worth 24% of civil servants' salaries, split between the RGC as employer (18%) and employees (6%). However, this has yet to be implemented. The NSSF-C is autonomous but is supervised (and financed) by the MoSVY. The NFV is supervised by the MoSVY too. Both schemes have their own boards of directors, which include the MoEF and the MoSVY.

The SPPF commits to assessing the possibility of operating a pension scheme for workers and employees covered by the Labour Law. Private sector pension provisions are also included in the strategic plan for the Financial Sector Development Strategy 2011-2020 (FSDS). This scheme would include old-age pensions, old-age allowances, invalidity pensions, survivors' pensions and beneficiary allowances (RGC, 2011b). According to the FSDS, the scheme will entitle NSSF members who are 55 years and older to an old-age pension if they have registered with the NSSF in the last 20 years and paid the contribution for at least 60 months within the last 10 years.

Including the NSSF-C and NFV, about 5.1% of households with at least one elderly individual (defined as at least 60 years old) reported having received a pension transfer in 2014, up from 4.4% in 2009 (NIS, 2014, 2009). The NSDP (2014-2018) provides summary indicators on both social insurance coverage and social welfare programmes. The coverage trends (actual and projected) for the NSSF-C and NFV (Figure 2.3) reflect the impact of demographic change and the RGC's plans to expand coverage to all civil servants.

Figure 2.3. **Social insurance coverage is growing as the number of civil servants increases**

Social insurance coverage in Cambodia, select programmes (2013-18)

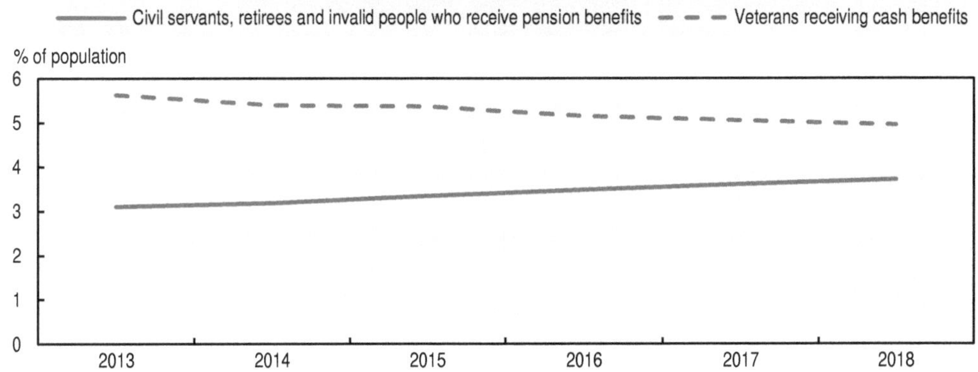

Source: MoP (2014), *National Strategic Development Plan (NDSP) 2014-2018*, available at *mop.gov.kh/Home/NSDP/NSDP20142018/tabid/216/Default.aspx*.

Replacement rates for retired civil servants are calculated with respect to their basic salary rather than total remuneration. This basic salary accounts for 58% of total remuneration; the balance consists of allowances and risk-related payments. As a result, pensions are low in absolute terms even though replacement rates appear to be high: employees with 30 or more years of service are entitled to a monthly benefit equivalent to 80% of their basic monthly salary, while the replacement rate for those who have worked for between 20 and 30 years ranges from 60% to 80%. Retirement ages vary depending on the history of employment, and are set at 60 for grade A employees, 58 for grade B and 55 for grade C.

Civil servants who lose the ability to work while on duty are entitled to 50-95% of their basic salary. The entitlement for their dependants is set at USD 1.25 per month per child and a slightly higher amount for surviving spouses (ILO, 2012a). The NSSF-C indexes all pension benefits to civil servant wages.

Occupational injury and health coverage

Workers in private-sector companies employing eight or more individuals have been covered by Employment Injury Insurance (EII) since 2008. This arrangement is financed through employer contributions to the National Social Security Fund (NSSF) equivalent to 0.8% of an employee's salary. EII provides healthcare coverage in the event of injury or illness related to work or following traffic accidents (if suffered on the way to or from work).

The NSSF also pays a benefit equivalent to 70% of a worker's salary in the event of a temporary disability. In the case of a permanent disability, the level of the benefit depends on the degree of disability and a worker's age. If an accident or illness results in the death of a worker, the EII covers funeral costs and provides a benefit to dependants. The EII replaced the previous dispensation whereby employers were directly responsible for medical costs and foregone wages associated with a workplace accident or illness.

The NSSF is responsible for registering formal sector enterprises, collecting contributions and co-ordinating the provision of health services and other benefits to members. The NSSF also issues the required identification code and membership cards to member employers and their employees. Employers are required to provide individual payroll information, including the monthly wage of each employee, to the NSSF and to report any cases of employment injuries no later than 48 hours after they witness or receive information about the incident.[6]

As of 2014, 7 041 enterprises were registered with the NSSF and 1.02 million workers were covered, versus 483 487 workers in 2010. Garment factory workers account for the largest share of the covered population, followed by hospitality workers, who are largely concentrated in Phnom Penh (Hennicot, 2012). In 2015, employers reported 27 916 cases to the NSSF, which disbursed approximately USD 3 million that year, representing a 50% increase in benefit payments from 2014.

According to the Social Protection Strategy for Persons Defined by the Provisions of the Labour Law for the period 2014-2018, the EII faces a number of challenges relating to compliance by employers and employees not possessing the right documentation. Employees have expressed concerns about the quality of health services provided through EII mechanisms.

Social health insurance

The RGC has only recently established a framework for social health insurance, but coverage is growing rapidly. In 2009, the RGC collaborated with Groupe de recherches et d'échanges technologiques (GRET), a French non-governmental organisation,[7] to implement a Health Insurance Project (HIP), with financial support from Agence Française de Développement (AFD). The programme was mainly piloted in garment factories to inform its expansion nationally.

Box 2.2. **The NSSF can serve as the basis for social insurance in the future**

The NSSF was formally established by sub-decree in 2007 under the authority of the MoLVT for technical matters and under the MoEF for financial issues. The NSSF is presently responsible for managing the EII and social health insurance. However, it has been envisaged as the basis for a system of social insurance for private-sector workers since the Law on Social Security Schemes for Persons Defined by the Provisions of the Labour Law in 2002. This legislation empowered the NSSF, a public enterprise, to manage pension and occupational health arrangements, as well as social security mechanisms for "other contingencies".

The Social Protection Strategy for Persons Defined by the Provisions of the Labour Law for the period 2014-2018 establishes four goals for the NSSF, which are reflected in the SPPF:

1. Extending and strengthening the implementation of the employment injury insurance
2. Implementing the processing of the health insurance scheme
3. Implementing the processing of the pension scheme
4. Strengthening governance

The NSSF can build on its success in registering enterprises for the EII in promoting coverage of other social security arrangements. However, the exclusion of businesses that employ fewer than eight individuals means that only a small minority of the workforce will be covered. According to the 2011 Enterprise Census, 80% of enterprises employ just one or two individuals.

In 2013, the MoLVT and the MoEF approved a social health insurance (SHI) roadmap that integrates the Health Insurance Project (HIP) within the NSSF. By the end of 2015, the HIP had registered 11 factories and almost 8 000 employees. In March 2016, the MoLVT launched SHI in two phases: phase one covers members registered for SHI and victims of work injury and their dependants; phase two covers dependants of SHI members. SHI became operational in December 2016 and will at first only cover Phnom Penh and two provinces: Kandal and Kampong Speu (MoLVT, 2016).

Prakas No. 109 of 2016 defines the SHI health benefits and preventive services to be provided by the NSSF. Prakas No. 220 of 2016 specifies the contribution rates for SHI. Contributions are divided equally between employer and employee, with each contributing to the NSSF at a rate of 1.3% of the employee's salary.

Health insurance arrangements for workers outside the NSSF remain limited. However, a royal decree paving the way for health insurance for civil servants has been issued and is expected to take effect in 2017. Private health insurance schemes have become more common since the Insurance Law of 2000 was passed but they are affordable only to higher income earners.

TVET programmes are the main labour market interventions but coverage is low

Labour market policies have been a feature of Cambodia's social protection landscape since the late 1990s, but they have evolved as the needs of the country have changed. Their emphasis has gradually shifted from public works programmes, with a clear focus on poverty alleviation and rural development appropriate for the early years of national reconstruction, to initiatives designed to improve workers' skills and the quality of work. These programmes are suitable in a context where labour participation is high but productivity levels are low, and where a significant skills mismatch exists between the supply and demand for labour.

Technical vocational education and training (TVET) programmes are the most important labour market policy. TVET provides skills training to individuals of working age (18-59) in informal employment who dropped out of secondary school below grade 10 which make up 21.1% of the population in 2014. The MoLVT is the main agency responsible for TVET[8] and is supported in this by donor partners. There are two types of TVET: short/non-certificate courses (one week to four months) and long-term/formal courses (one year or longer). Small loans are also granted for successful TVET participants.[9]

TVET coverage is low given the size of the informal sector and productivity levels in Cambodia. The programme covers around 1.3% of the target population, or 43 000 beneficiaries, per year. The ADB is working with the MoLVT on extending the programme nationwide, improving the quality of the training, introducing formal certification and strengthening the linkages with employers.

TVET courses cover a broad range of sectors, including construction, auto mechanics, electrical works, manufacturing, crop planting and harvesting, food processing and hairdressing. The short course is among the initiatives most aligned to core social protection objectives. Programme authorities select candidates according to IDPoor status and recommendations by local authorities and school administrators. Individuals who complete the training are eligible for microcredit through the Self-Employment Generation Fund and other sources.

The National Employment Policy (NEP) is one of three specific policies through which Cambodia's active labour market policies (ALMPs) will be implemented (RGC, 2015) and is intended to improve the employment prospects of the estimated 300 000 young people entering the labour market every year

(MoLVT, 2013). The NEP, which covers the period 2015-25, was adopted by the RGC in 2015. It has three main objectives: i) increase decent and productive employment opportunities; ii) enhance skills and human resource development; and iii) enhance labour market governance.

Although no data are available to evaluate the impact of TVET, its benefits for participants are likely to be significant, given the characteristics of the Cambodian labour market and in the context of high school drop-out rates. Programmes such as TVET provide an important avenue for skills development, allowing individuals to move into more productive sectors of the economy. TVET schemes are likely a high-return investment, with the potential added benefit of supporting structural transformation. Going forward, TVET schemes should be evaluated to determine their effectiveness.

The National Youth Development Policy (NYDP) recognises youth empowerment as an urgent and cross-sectoral concern. Adopted in 2011, the NYDP places a strong emphasis on employment, education and skills training, and health and youth participation. Rather than establish new policies, the NYDP connects and co-ordinates existing sectoral policies, plans skills-development initiatives that address shortages in skilled labour, such as second chance education, student loans and community centres for youth who drop out or who have a disability. An operational plan (the National Youth Action Plan) is currently being finalised for the NYDP with the aim of better connecting youth with the labour market through employment services and entrepreneurship initiatives (MoEYS, 2015).

The number of TVET graduates tripled from 2009 to 2013, with about 350 000 participants attending training, 93 220 in the academic year 2012/13 alone (MoLVT, 2013). In addition, the MoEYS, with support from donor partners, has implemented various life skills programmes and continuous learning projects for school drop-outs.[10] At least 50 international and local NGOs work to promote youth education, with a particular focus on the most vulnerable and disadvantaged (UNDP, 2009). The MoEYS has also run TVET programmes through three secondary level technical schools.

The CfW and FfW programmes build on a long series of public works schemes. The WFP has implemented public works programmes in Cambodia under the auspices of the FfW programme since the 1990s. Other food-for-work public works programmes are donor-funded, fragmented and small in scale. Donor partners run over 500 such projects each year as part of rural development initiatives but there exists very little information about them.[11]

The CfW programme has two phases. In its first phase, the programme complements machine-based works with labour-based soil works, improving tertiary canals and roads. In its second phase, it provides resources for agriculture, including working capital and some longer-term investments, such as irrigation pumps, seeds and fertilisers. The CfW programme has created over 2 million work days[12] in a three-year cycle and has run over 400 projects, ranging from rural road development to irrigation canals. Such projects not only create jobs but also serve to build or rehabilitate rural infrastructure, thereby improving access to essential services and boosting agricultural production (MoEF, 2015).

There is no statutory unemployment insurance scheme in Cambodia. Workers employed on contracts of unspecified duration who are dismissed after at least six months of employment for a reason other than serious misconduct are entitled to severance pay from their employer. The quantum of severance pay depends on the worker's salary and length of service. For employment of between six months and a year, workers are entitled to a payment equivalent to seven days of wages and benefits. This rises to 15 days for employment longer than one year, 20 days for more than two years and so on up to a maximum of six months for employment of 20 years or more.

Contract employees are also entitled to severance pay. The exact amount of the severance pay is set by a collective agreement and must be equal to or greater than 5% of the total wages paid during the length of the contract, if no such agreement exists (RGC, 1997).

Women's right to maternity leave is codified in the Labour Law. Employers are statutorily obliged to provide 90 days of maternity leave to employees who give birth; such workers cannot be dismissed while on maternity leave or just before departing on maternity leave (RGC, 1997). Women who have been employed for a year or more with their current employer are entitled to receive half their pay and benefits while on maternity leave. Meanwhile, men are entitled to one day of paternity leave from their employer.

Maternity-related provisions extend beyond maternity leave. For the first two months after returning to work, employers should by law only expect women to perform light work, and for one year from the date of child delivery, mothers who breast-feed their children are entitled to one hour per day during working hours to do so. An enterprise employing 100 or more women must establish a day-care centre within their establishment or nearby for children between the ages of 18 months and three years. The ILO has found a high level of compliance with maternity-related legislation among companies in the garment and footwear sector (ILO, 2012b). However, informal-sector workers are very unlikely to receive the same protection.

Notes

1. Consultations with the MoSVY, 27 February 2016.
2. Sub-Decree No. 291 ANKr. BK, 27 December 2011. See *idpoor.gov.kh/Data/En/Reference/IDPoor_SubDecree_Eng-FINAL.pdf*.

3. See the GIZ (2016) powerpoint on the IDPoor process in urban areas.
4. Adverse selection refers to the phenomenon of individuals expecting high health care costs being more likely to enrol or preferring more generous insurance plans than healthier individuals, resulting in issues of risk pooling.
5. The NSSF-C and NFV were established in accordance with the Law on the Common Statute of Civil Servants (1994), Sub-Decree No. 59 (1997) and Sub-Decree No. 14 (2008). The Law on (Old-age) Pensions and Invalidity Pensions for Soldiers of the Armed Forces, Law on War Veterans, National Disability Law and the Insurance Law all align with provisions under the NSSF-C and the NFV (ILO, 2012).
6. See the NSSF website at *nssf.gov.kh/default/language/en/*.
7. An international development NGO governed by French law.
8. Until 2004, TVET was overseen by the MoEYS. In 2005, this oversight was moved to the MoLVT, although the MoEYS still retains some involvement in TVET through secondary education technical schools. Even the MoWA has been involved in delivering some kinds of TVET for women (World Bank, 2010).
9. Consultation with the MoLVT, 24 February 2016.
10. Interviews with a MoEYS official, February 2015. Few concrete details on actual activities are available.
11. See Annex 2.A1 for an inventory of several such social programmes.
12. Consultation with the MoEF, 2016.

References

Annear, P.L. et al. (2016), "National coverage and health service utilization by Health Equity Fund members, 2004–2015", Australian Development Research Award Research Report.

Bigdeli, M. and P.L. Annear (2009), "Barriers to access and the purchasing function of health equity funds: lessons from Cambodia", *Bulletin of the World Health Organization*, No. 87, pp. 560-564, Geneva, *http://dx.doi.org/10.2471/BLT.08.053058*.

Bigdeli, M. et al. (2016), "Access to Treatment for Diabetes and Hypertension in Rural Cambodia: Performance of Existing Social Health Protection Schemes", PLoS ONE, Vol. 11, Issue 1, *http://dx.doi.org/10.1371/journal.pone.0146147*.

CARD (2010), "Toward the Social Protection Strategy for the poor and vulnerable in Cambodia", Background Paper for Cambodia Development Cooperation Forum – III, CDC – 2-3 June 2010, Council for Agricultural and Rural Development, Royal Government of Cambodia, Phnom Penh, *cdc-crdb.gov.kh/cdc/third_cdcf/session2/social_protection_for_%20the_poor_and_vulnerable/card_background_paper_on_nsps_en.htm*

Chantum, C. (2012), "Building resilience and opportunity: The role of labor and social assistance policies", Session: Technology for Implementation, Building Resilience and Opportunity: The Role of Labor and Social Assistance Policies South-South Learning Forum, 30 October - 3 November 2012, Hyderabad, India.

Ensor, T. et al. (2017), "Impact of health financing policies in Cambodia: A 20 year experience", *Social Science & Medicine*, Vol. 177, pp. 118–126, *https://dx.doi.org/10.1016/j.socscimed.2017.01.034*.

Fernandes Antunes, A. and B. Jacobs (2014), "Access to Public Health Services: Why Do Eligible Households Not Make Use of Health Equity Fund Benefits?", Briefings for Health Financing Policy-Making in Cambodia, No. 3, GIZ, Phnom Penh, *giz-cambodia.com/wordpress/wp-content/uploads/Briefing-note-3-HEF-non-utilisation-EN.pdf* (accessed 30 July 2017).

Filmer, D. and N. Schady (2009), "School enrolment, selection and test scores", *World Bank Policy Research Working Paper*, No. 4998, World Bank, Washington, DC, *http://dx.doi.org/10.1596/1813-9450-4998*.

Flores, G. et al. (2013), "Financial protection of patients through compensation of providers: The impact of health equity funds in Cambodia", *Journal of Health Economics* 32(6), pp. 1180-1193, *http://dx.doi.org/10.1016/j.jhealeco.2013.09.012*.

GIZ (2016), "Urban IDPoor in a nutshell", Deutsche Gesellschaft für Internationale Zusammenarbeit (GIZ) IDPoor team, Phnom Penh, 25 February 2016, powerpoint presentation.

HelpAge International (2010), "Older People's associations Rolled Out across Cambodia", webpage, HelpAge International, London, *helpage.org/newsroom/latest-news/older-peoples-associations-rolled-out-across-cambodia/* (accessed 8 April 2016).

Hennicot, J.C. (2012), *Actuarial Review of the NSSF Employment Injury Branch and Assessment of Social Health Insurance*, Deutsche Gesellschaft für Internationale Zusammenarbeit (GIZ), Phnom Penh, *giz-cambodia.com/wordpress/wp-content/uploads/Actuarial-Review-of-The-NSSF-Employment-Injury-Branch-and-Assessment-of-....pdf*.

ILO (2012a), *Cambodia: Social Protection Expenditure and Performance Review*, International Labour Organization, Geneva, pp. 64-6, 82, *ilo.org/asia/whatwedo/publications/WCMS_216146/lang--en/index.htm*.

ILO (2012b), *Practical challenges for maternity protection in the Cambodian garment industry*, International Labour Organization, Geneva, *ilo.org/wcmsp5/groups/public/---asia/---ro-bangkok/---sro-bangkok/documents/publication/wcms_203802.pdf*.

MoEF (forthcoming), *Social Protection Policy Framework*, Draft by Ernst and Young, Royal Government of Cambodia, Phnom Penh.

MoEF (2015), *An Assessment of Cash for Work Program Under EFAP-AF*, Ministry of Economy and Finance, Royal Government of Cambodia, Phnom Penh.

MoEYS (2015), *National Youth Action Plan*, Draft, Ministry of Education, Youth and Sport, Royal Government of Cambodia, Phnom Penh.

MoH (2008), *Health Strategic Plan 2008-2015*, Ministry of Health, Royal Government of Cambodia, Phnom Penh, *apps.who.int/medicinedocs/documents/s18360en/s18360en.pdf*

MoLVT (2016), *Annual Activity Report for 2015 and 2016*, Ministry of Labour and Vocational Training, Royal Government of Cambodia, Phnom Penh.

MoLVT (2013), *Strategic Planning and Development of Technical Vocational Education and Training 2014-2018*, Ministry of Labour and Vocational Training, Royal Government of Cambodia, Phnom Penh.

MoP (2014), *National Strategic Development Plan (NDSP) 2014-2018*, available at *mop.gov.kh/Home/NSDP/NSDP20142018/tabid/216/Default.aspx*.

NIS, MoH and ICF International (2015), *Cambodia Demographic Health Survey 2014*, Final Report, National Institute of Statistics and Directorate General for Health and ICF International, Phnom Penh, *dhsprogram.com/publications/publication-fr312-dhs-final-reports.cfm*.

NIS (2014), *Cambodia Socio-Economic Survey 2014*, National Institute of Statistics, Ministry of Planning, Royal Government of Cambodia, Phnom Penh.

NIS (2009), *Cambodia Socio-Economic Survey 2009, Household Survey 2009*, National Institute of Statistics, Ministry of Planning, Royal Government of Cambodia, Phnom Penh.

NIS (2004), *Cambodia Socio-Economic Survey 2004, Household Survey 2004*, National Institute of Statistics, Ministry of Planning, Royal Government of Cambodia, Phnom Penh.

People in Need and UNICEF (2014), *Phnom Penh: Multiple Indicator Assessment of the Urban Poor*, People in Need and United Nations Children's Fund, Phnom Penh, *unicef.org/cambodia/PIN_URBAN_POOR_FA.pdf*.

RGC (2016), *Strategy of Social Protection System Development 2016-2025*, Draft, March 2016, Royal Government of Cambodia, Phnom Penh.

RGC (2015), *National Employment Policy*, Royal Government of Cambodia, Phnom Penh.

RGC (2014), *Policy on Labour Migration for Cambodia*, Royal Government of Cambodia, Phnom Penh, *colomboprocess.org/images/pdfs/Labour_Migration_Policy_for_Cambodia_2015-18.pdf*.

RGC (2011a), *The National Social Protection Strategy for the Poor and Vulnerable: Process of Development*, Royal Government of Cambodia, Phnom Penh, *unicef.org/cambodia/National_Social_Protection_Strategy_for_the_Poor_and_Vulnerable_Eng.pdf*.

RGC (2011b), *Financial Sector Development Strategy 2011-2020*, Royal Government of Cambodia, Phnom Penh, *pcspgroup.com/customers_demo/ngo_forum/website/files-tinymce/New_Pic/Development_Policies/Sectoral_Policies/Financial_Sector_Development_Strategy_2011-2020_Eng.pdf*.

RGC (1997), "Royal Kram CS/RKM/0397/01 promulgating the Labour Law", Labour Law, Royal Government of Cambodia, Phnom Penh, *ilo.org/dyn/natlex/natlex4.detail?p_lang=en&p_isn=46560&p_country=KHM&p_count=175&p_classification=01.02&p_classcount=2*

UNDP (2009), *Situation Analysis of Youth in Cambodia*, United Nations Development Programme, Phnom Penh, *unicef.org/cambodia/results_for_children_13004.htm*.

Van Minh, H. et al. (2014), "Progress toward universal health coverage in ASEAN", *Global Health Action*, Vol. 7, pp. 1-13, *http://dx.doi.org/10.3402/gha.v7.25856*.

UNICEF (2016), *Mapping of Residential Care Institutions*, United Nations Children's Fund, New York, *unicef.org/cambodia/MAPPING_REPORT_5_provinces_ENG.pdf*.

UNICEF (2011), *With the Best Intentions: A Study of Attitudes Towards Residential Care in Cambodia*, United Nations Children's Fund, New York, *unicef.org/eapro/Study_Attitudes_towards_RC.pdf*.

WHO (2015), *The Kingdom of Cambodia Health System Review*, Health Systems in Transition, Vol. 5, No. 2, World Health Organization, Geneva, *wpro.who.int/asia_pacific_observatory/hits/series/cambodia_health_systems_review.pdf*.

WHO (2010), *Health systems financing: the path to universal coverage*, World Health Report 2010, World Health Organization, Geneva, *who.int/whr/2010/en*.

World Bank (2015), *The State of Social Safety Nets 2015*, World Bank, Washington, DC, *documents.worldbank.org/curated/en/415491467994645020/The-state-of-social-safety-nets-2015*.

World Bank (2010), "Providing skills for equity and growth: Preparing Cambodia's youth for the labor market", Working Paper, World Bank, Washington, DC, *documents.worldbank.org/curated/en/207001468232481313/pdf/599890REVISED00Edited0skills0report.pdf*.

ANNEX 2.A1.

Inventory of Cambodia's social protection programmes

Table 2.A1.1. **Social assistance programmes for emergency response**

Category	Programme/Scheme	Type and value of transfer	Eligibility	Coverage	Ministry/Agency
Emergency	Emergency Food Assistance Project	Food; ..	Food insecure households: IDPoor 1 and 2 affected by food price crisis	Beneficiaries: 500 000 Provinces: 10 Districts: 33 Communes: 100	Ministry of Economy and Finance (MoEF)
	Food Reserve System	Food; ..	Food insecure households affected by natural disasters	Nationwide	MoEF/ National Committee for Disaster Management
	Social interventions for emergency and relief	Food; ..	Households affected by natural disaster and other vulnerabilities	Provinces: 2 Beneficiaries: approximately 15 000	Ministry of Social Affairs, Veterans and Youth Rehabilitation (MoSVY)
	Cash-for-work programme	Cash; on average USD 5 per work day	Food insecure households affected by natural disasters	The first phase of the programme (ended in 2012), created 2 million work days; sustaining temporary jobs in a three-year cycle	MoEF
	Reducing the vulnerability of rural Cambodian livelihoods through enhanced sub-national climate change planning and execution of priority actions	Cash; ..	Poor households	Provinces: 2 Beneficiaries: close to 15 000, about 4 000 of whom are poor/ vulnerable women	MoE/Secretariat of the National Committee for Democratic Development, (NCDD-S)

Table 2.A1.1. **Social assistance programmes for emergency response** *(cont.)*

Category	Programme/Scheme	Type and value of transfer	Eligibility	Coverage	Ministry/Agency
Human development	Cash transfer for poor families with pregnant mothers/children under five years (U5)	Cash; ..	Pregnant women and U5 children	Women: 2 145 Children: 1 200	NCDD-S/ Council of Agricultural and Rural Development (CARD)
	NOURISH Mother/Child nutrition cash transfer incentive for health service utilisation	Cash; ..	Pregnant women and U2 children	Provinces: 3 Beneficiaries: 300 000	Save the Children District/municipality/ commune
	School food programme	Food; ..	All students in selected schools in rural/remote areas with food insecurity	Provinces: 9 Schools: 1 219 Students: 300 000	Ministry of Education, Youth and Sport (MoEYS)
	Primary school take-home rations	Food; ..	Students in grades 4-6 IDPoor 1 and 2	Provinces: 3 Schools: 765 Students: 6 200	MoEYS
	Home-grown school feeding	Food-for-work/ cash-for-work programme; ..	All students in grades 1-6 in selected schools in rural/remote areas with food insecurity	Schools: 59 Students: 13 000	MoEYS
	Primary school scholarships	Cash; USD 60 per year	Students in grades 4-6 in schools in rural/remote areas IDPoor 1 and 2	Nationwide Schools: 2 934 Students: 79 004 (planned), 77 605 (actual)	MoEYS
	Primary school scholarships	Cash; USD 60 per year	Students in grades 4-6 in schools in rural/remote areas IDPoor 1 and 2	Students: 26 000 (Different areas than the RGC primary school scholarships)	MoEYS
	Lower secondary scholarships	Cash; USD 60 per year	Students in grades 7-9 from poor households	Schools: 809 (out of 1 600) Students: 70 574	MoEYS
	Upper Secondary Scholarship	Cash; USD 90 per year	Students in grades 10-12 from poor households (currently covering only grade 10)	Schools: 120 Students: 3 600	MoEYS
Social health protection	Health Equity Fund(s)	Fee subsidy; ..	Members of poor households with IDPoor cards	Nationwide Recipients: 2.9 million	Ministry of Health (MoH)
	Community-based health insurance	Insurance benefit; ..	Poor and near poverty	Operating Districts (ODs): 21 Members: 117 726	MoH/ Non-governmental organisations (NGOs)
	Voucher for reproductive health scheme	Health service; ..	Women and children from poor families	Provinces: 5 ODs: 23 Cases: 68 276	MoH

Table 2.A1.1. **Social assistance programmes for emergency response** *(cont.)*

Category	Programme/Scheme	Type and value of transfer	Eligibility	Coverage	Ministry/Agency
Vulnerable groups	Social welfare for the elderly	-	Elderly (65+ years)	Provinces: 11 Associations: 358	MoSVY
	Social welfare for families living with disabilities	-	People with disabilities who are poor, elderly or have no supporting families	Beneficiaries: 300 000 (almost 100% coverage)	MoSVY
	Disability allowance	Cash; USD 5 per month	People with disabilities who are poor, elderly or have no supporting families, verified by local authorities	Nominally nationwide	MoSVY
	Social welfare for vulnerable children and orphans	Social service; USD 1.25 per day per child	Vulnerable children and children living in residential care institutions	Nationwide Institutions: 253 Children: 11 017 (to include only the RGC)	MoSVY/ NGOs

Notes: .. = Missing value or not available; - = Absolute zero
* Per year, unless otherwise noted.
** USD = United States dollar; KHR = Cambodian riel.

Table 2.A1.2. **Social protection programmes for labour market policy and employment**

Category	Programme/Scheme	Type and cost of transfer	Eligibility	Coverage	Ministry/Agency
Labour policy and employment	Second chance or informal technical vocational education and training (TVET)	Training; USD* 28 for one week, USD 100 for one year	Young drop-outs from poor households, referred by local and school authority	Nationwide, which includes 36 training institutions, 12 NGO-run training centres, 750 private providers, and 100 000 expected participants	Ministry of Labour and Vocational Training (MoLVT)

* USD = United States dollar.

Table 2.A1.3. **Social insurance schemes summary matrix**

Category	Programme/ Scheme	Type and value of transfer	Eligibility	Coverage	Ministry/ Agency
Old-age pension	National Social Security Fund for Civil Servants (NSSF-C)/ National Fund for Veterans (NFV)	Cash; the minimum benefit is 60% of the final basic salary and allowances (excluding position allowance). The maximum benefit is 80% of final salary for 30 years of service The pension amount is subject to a minimum amount, depending on the salary grade. Retirement allowance is equal to eight months of total final salary	Lifetime pension payable after 20 years of service (minimum) at the normal retirement age of 55 NSSF-C: civil servants, excluding police and armed forces NFV: war veterans, police and armed forces	NSSF-C recipients: about 180 000 civil servants and their dependents NFV recipients: about 87 500 war veterans, police and armed forces and their dependents	MoSVY

Table 2.A1.3. **Social insurance schemes summary matrix** *(cont.)*

Category	Programme/ Scheme	Type and value of transfer	Eligibility	Coverage	Ministry/ Agency
Invalidity	NSSF-C and NFV	Cash; the minimum benefit is 50% of final salary and allowances (not including position allowance). The maximum benefit is 65% of final salary for 30 years of service The pension amount is subject to a minimum amount, depending on the salary grade. For less than 20 years of service, a lump sum benefit is payable equal to four to ten months of total final salary Invalidity allowance is payable equal to six months of total final salary	Lifetime pension payable after 20 years of service (minimum)	NSSF-C recipients: about 180 000 civil servants and their dependents NFV recipients: about 87 500 war veterans, police and armed forces and their dependents	MoSVY
	NSSF (EII)	Cash; a contribution of 3% from employees and 0.8% from employers	Employees of business enterprises with at least eight employees	Enterprises: 7 796 Employees: 1.1 million	MoLVT
Health insurance	NSSF-C and NFV	Insurance benefit	NSSF-C: civil servants, excluding police and armed forces NFV: war veterans, police and armed forces	NSSF-C recipients: about 180 000 civil servants and their dependents NFV: about 87 500 war veterans, police and armed forces and their dependents	MoSVY
	NSSF	Insurance benefit; a proposed contribution of 50% from employees and 50% from employers A contribution rate of 2.4% of insurable earning for medical care and 1.4% for sickness cash benefits and maternity cash benefits	Employees of business enterprises with at least eight employees	Enterprises: 11 Employees: 7 956 (as of 2015)	MoLVT

* KHR = Cambodian riel; USD = Unites States dollar.

Source: ILO (2012a).

Table 2.A1.4. **Other social protection programmes by NSSF-C and NFV**

Benefit type	Benefit details
Sickness cash benefit	Full salary, including allowances for up to three consecutive months of illness and 90% of salary thereafter for up to 12 months, depending on years of service
Maternity benefits	Maternity leave for 90 days at full salary and cash allowance of KHR* 600 000 per child or miscarriage
Marriage allowance	A cash allowance payable at first marriage
Work injury benefits	Medical care, cash benefit at full salary during treatment and convalescence, and permanent invalidity benefits for permanent disability
Death benefits in case of death on mission	Cash allowance of six months of total final salary of the deceased Funeral allowance Survivor pension payable to widow at KHR 6 000 per month and KHR 5 000 per month for each child under 16 years
Death benefits in case of civilian death	Funeral allowance of 12 months of pension of the deceased Survivor pension payable to widow at KHR 6 000 per month and KHR 5 000 per month for each child under 16 years

* KHR = Cambodian riel.

ANNEX 2.A2.

Rural IDPoor: Indicators and identification process

As of 2012, the rural IDPoor Programme methodology has used the following household poverty indicators:

- Housing conditions, including roof, wall, area, house quality and home ownership;
- Size of legally owned residential land and productive agricultural land;
- Main source of income from growing crops, fishing or other activities;
- Animal husbandry, including fish farming;
- Ability to meet food requirements;
- Number of members unable to earn an income relative to total number of members;
- Material goods and equipment;
- Means of transportation;
- Unexpected problems or crises that cause lost income, food shortages, sale of property or incursion of debt;
- Number of children aged 6 to 11 years who missed school and the reasons why;
- Situations that can deteriorate living conditions, such as household head suffering serious disability or chronic disease, exclusively elderly members, live-in orphans, female-headed households with many young children, no members with the capacity to work;
- Situations that can improve living conditions, such as assistance from relatives or other sources of income.

According to the Ministry of Planning, the process for identification of poor households consists of the following seven steps:

Step 1: Establish and train the Planning and Budgeting Committee Representative Group (PBCRG) at the commune level;

Step 2: Establish and train Village Representative Groups (VRGs);

Step 3: VRG compiles list of households in the village, conducts household interviews, considers special circumstances of households; and after a Commune Review Meeting, compiles and publicly displays the first draft list of poor households in the village;

Step 4: VRG conducts village consultation meeting on first draft list of poor households, receives complaints, prepares and displays final draft list of poor households, and submits the list to the Commune Council;

Step 5: Commune Council reviews and approves final list of poor households, sends data to Provincial Department of Planning; and distributes Equity Cards to poor households (after data entry and photography in Steps 6 and 7);

Step 6: Provincial Department of Planning enters all data and household photos into provincial database of poor households;

Step 7: Photography of poor households.

Chapter 3

The pro-poor potential of social protection and fiscal policy

This chapter focuses on the impact of existing social protection programmes on poverty and inequality. It finds that social assistance in Cambodia is well targeted through the IDPoor system but has little impact on poverty and inequality because of low levels of coverage and low benefit levels. Health Equity Funds, however, do ease the burden of health spending for a significant number of poor households. Pension benefits for retired civil servants and military veterans dominate social protection spending and are unsustainable. Social protection spending in Cambodia is low by regional standards. The tax system is progressive but increases poverty, an impact that public transfers are too small to offset.

The previous chapters examined the needs for social protection in Cambodia's fast-changing society (Chapter 1) and discussed the extent to which the country's current social protection system is aligned to the needs of the population of today and tomorrow (Chapter 2). This chapter focuses on the impact of the existing social protection programmes on poverty and inequality. In doing so, it will not only examine the main social protection programmes but also analyse the way these policies are financed, since both aspects are likely to affect social policy outcomes.

Social assistance is undermined by low coverage

The low coverage of social assistance programmes means that the sector currently has little impact in terms of reducing poverty or inequality at a national level. Figure 3.1 shows coverage rates for scholarship programmes acquired from CSES data (distinguishing between those that are administered by the Royal Government of Cambodia (RGC) and those which are not). No quintile has a coverage rate higher than 2%.

The level of benefits is also not high: the value of the scholarship, USD 60 per year, equates to just 10.8% of the national poverty gap. However, it should be noted that this benefit level would be more than enough to close the poverty gap if received universally, reflecting the diminished severity of poverty between 2004 and 2014.

Technical vocational education and training (TVET), meanwhile, accounted for 16% of individuals currently attending an educational facility in 2014. There are no data for estimating the incidence of TVET coverage, though it is important to note that its targeting criteria relate to educational attainment and sector of employment rather than income. Figure 3.2 estimates TVET coverage across the income distribution based on microsimulation analysis. Given the size of the informal sector in Cambodia, there is no marked difference in coverage rates across deciles.

Figure 3.1. **Scholarship coverage is lowest for students from the poorest households**

Incidence of scholarship beneficiaries among urban and rural households by income quintile in Cambodia (2014)

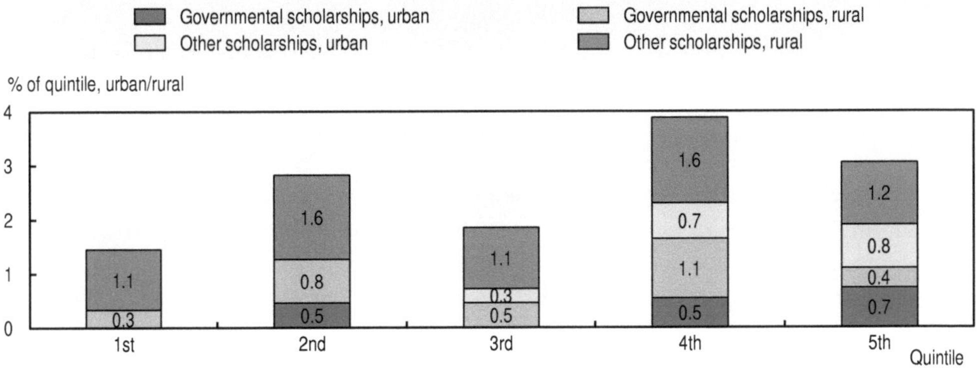

Note: The sample used for the government scholarships and other scholarships are households with school-attending children. Therefore, quintiles of household consumption in 2014 Cambodian riel (KHR) are defined according to the following cut-offs: 698 791 / 938 771 / 1 218 666 / 1 688 181.

Source: Authors' calculations based on NIS (2014), *Cambodia Socio-Economic Survey 2014.*

Figure 3.2. **Individuals across the income distribution make use of TVET programmes**

TVET coverage by household consumption decile in Cambodia (2014)

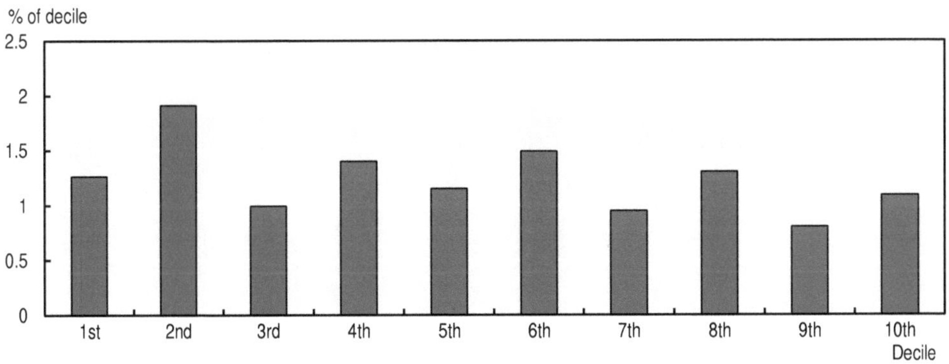

Note: The deciles of household consumption in 2014 Cambodian riel (KHR) are defined according to the following cut-offs: 350 282 / 456 077 / 549 250 / 636 399 / 729 553 / 829 604 / 961 286 / 1 137 181 / 1 495 614.

Source: Authors' calculations based on NIS (2014), *Cambodia Socio-Economic Survey 2014.*

Health spending is pro-poor and coverage is growing

In 2014, 8.3% of the population reported having benefited from free or subsidised health care (Figure 3.3) (NIS, 2014). In practical terms, this indicates the extent of coverage by Health Equity Funds (HEF), although a small number of those surveyed might have benefitted from fee exemptions or Kanta Bopha hospitals.[1] This coverage level corresponds with the findings of Flores et al. (2013), who state: "In areas in which a HEF was operating, 7.1% of households reported receipt of free or subsidised health care in the last 12 months, and a further 2.2% reported entitlement without receiving treatment. In areas with no HEF, the corresponding figures are 2.0% and 0.01%."

Nonetheless, the proportion of respondents who accessed free or subsidised healthcare is lower than HEF data indicate. This is likely to reflect the fact that people covered by HEF do not always use the public health facilities with whom HEF contracts (see Chapter 2).

In rural areas, the percentage of persons living in a household with access to subsidised health care is 9.2%, compared with 4.9% in urban areas. This finding is consistent with the fact that the Identification of Poor Households Programme (IDPoor) system targets rural areas. CSES data suggest a greater proportion of those with access to subsidised healthcare are women (52.7% versus 47.3% for men). Taking into account the gender of the household head, however, male-headed households report much greater access to free or subsidised health care: a rate of 68.8%, compared with 31.2% for female-headed households, which make up only 21.1% of all households.

Figure 3.3. **A majority of households do not have access to the HEF**
Share of households with access to free or subsidised health care in Cambodia (2014)

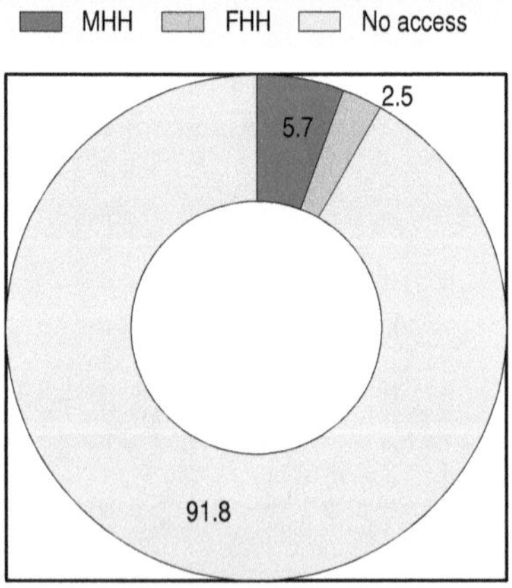

Note: MHH = male-headed household; FHH = female-headed household.
Source: Authors' calculations based on NIS (2014), *Cambodia Socio-Economic Survey 2014*.

The proportion of households reporting access to free or subsidised health care is highest among the first consumption quintile and decreases gradually to under 10% for the richest quintile (Figure 3.4). The first and second quintiles make up more than half of those who reported benefiting from free or subsidised health care. This finding is consistent with the good targeting performance of the IDPoor system. The CSES questionnaire specifies access at point-of-service during the previous 12 months alone, which may explain why self-reported coverage rates are not higher.

Figure 3.4. **Access to subsidised health care is highest for the poor**

Access to free or subsidised health care at point of service by consumption quintile in the last 12 months in Cambodia (2014)

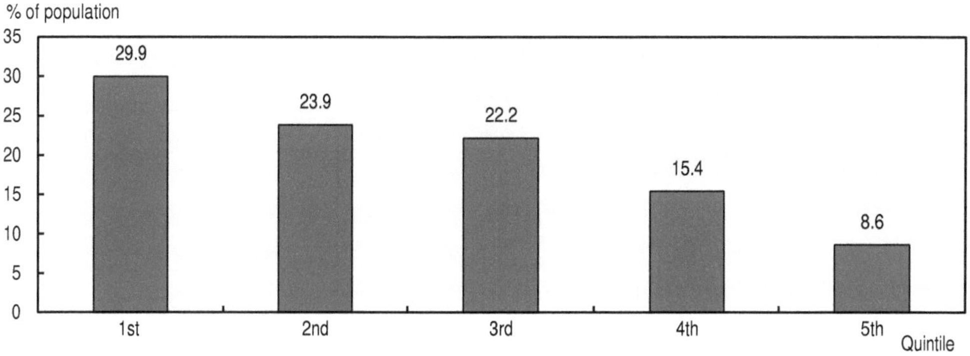

Note: The quintiles of household consumption in 2014 Cambodian riel (KHR) are defined according to the following cut-offs: 674 952 / 902 023 / 1 154 459 / 1 572 958 / 18 680 054.

Source: Authors' calculations based on NIS (2014), *Cambodia Socio-Economic Survey 2014*.

According to 2014 CSES data, out-of-pocket health expenditure rises with income. In the poorest consumption quintile, individual health expenditure ranged from minimum KHR 600 (Cambodian riel) (0.32% of the 2014 national poverty line) to maximum KHR 800 000 (428.71% of the 2014 national poverty line) (Figure 3.5). The weighted mean of out-of-pocket health expenditure for the first quintile in the 30 days preceding the survey was KHR 31 468 (16.8% of the 2014 national poverty line).

Figure 3.5. **Out-of-pocket health spending is highest for the richest households**

Out-of-pocket health expenditure by consumption quintile in the last 30 days in Cambodia, in KHR (2014)

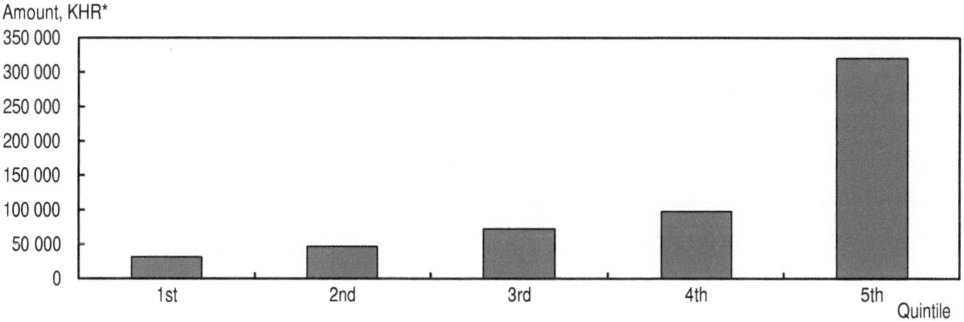

Note: The quintiles of household consumption in 2014 Cambodian riel (KHR) are defined according to the following cut-offs: 674 952 / 902 023 / 1 154 459 / 1 572 958 / 18 680 054.

Source: Authors' calculations based on NIS (2014), *Cambodia Socio-Economic Survey 2014*.

Catastrophic out-of-pocket health expenditure is much higher in rural areas. As captured by the 2014 CSES, 8.96% of households reported catastrophic health expenditure[2] in the 30 days preceding the survey, over 90% of which were in rural areas (Figure 3.6). This underlines the importance of social health protection in protecting all people against health shocks.

Figure 3.6. **Catastrophic out-of-pocket health expenditure affects a majority of households**

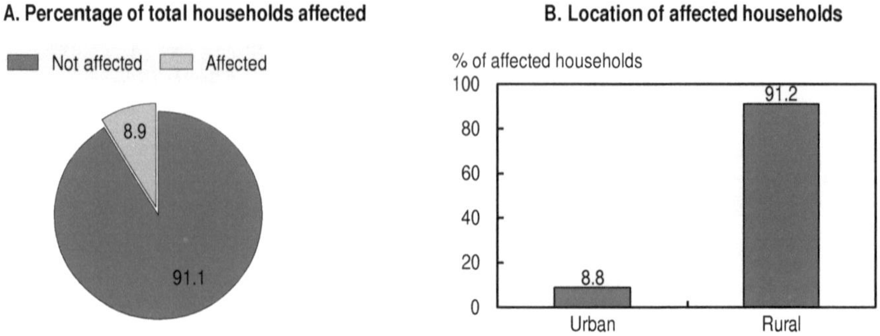

Source: Authors' calculations based on NIS (2014), *Cambodia Socio-Economic Survey 2014*, available at *nada-nis.gov.kh/index.php/catalog/CSES.*

Box 3.1. **Impact evaluation of health care micro-insurance in rural Cambodia**

The French NGO Groupe de recherches et d'échanges technologiques (GRET) launched a health care micro-insurance scheme, Sokapheap Krousat Yeugn (SKY), in 245 villages in the provinces of Takeo, Kandal and Kampot. From November 2007 to December 2008, the Agence française de développement (AFD) conducted an impact evaluation of the scheme which found that insurance was successful in helping families decrease their overall health expenditure (Levine et al., 2010).

SKY was estimated to decrease total health care costs of serious health shocks by over 40%. Households with coverage had more than one-third less debt and more than 75% less health-related debt, compared to households who did not have coverage. The scheme was also found to have changed health-seeking behaviour, increasing utilisation of insurance-covered public facilities and decreasing use of unregulated care, which was not covered by the scheme.

SKY had no detectable impact on preventive care, and there was little evidence of improvements in health outcomes. However, perceived or actual health care quality issues may have been at the root of that. The results remain important in developing more and better micro-insurance pilot programmes and methods of evaluating their impacts in Cambodia.

Public spending on social protection is low and not pro-poor

As Figure 3.7 shows, the RGC prioritised expenditure on the social sector[3] between 2009 and 2015. This sector received the largest allocation (4.5% of GDP in 2015) and showed the strongest growth over the survey period. The Ministries of Health and Education (MoH and MoEYS, respectively) combined accounted for just under 80% of total social spending on average between 2009 and 2015, while the Ministry of Social Affairs, Veterans and Youth Rehabilitation's (MoSVY) contribution increased from 13% to 19% over the same period. Economic sector[4] spending rose slightly between 2011 and 2015 but was only the fourth greatest expenditure after defence and general administration, which amounted to 3.2% and 1.9% of GDP in 2015, respectively.

Figure 3.7. **Social spending is high and rising**

Government spending by sector in Cambodia (2009-15)

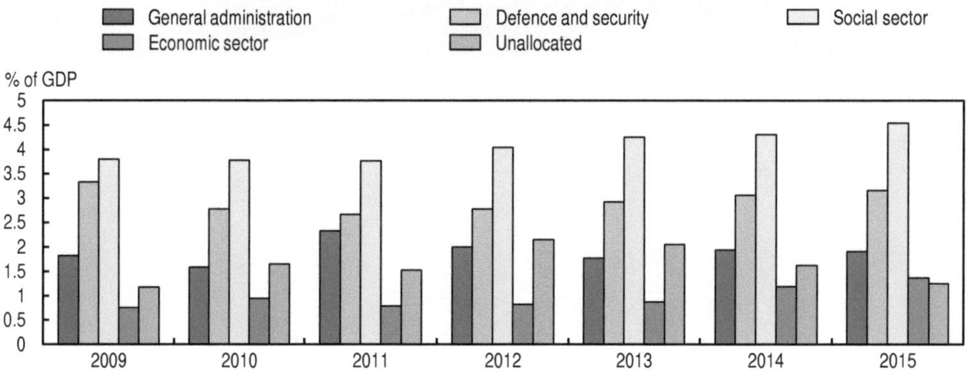

Source: Ministry of Economy and Finance (2016).

In 2016, transfers to the National Social Security Fund for Civil Servants (NSSF-C) and National Fund for Veterans (NFV) accounted for 88.8% of MoSVY's budget (Table 3.1). Of these two funds, the NFV absorbs the greater proportion despite the military being the smaller group. Both social insurance schemes are presently non-contributory (with no plan to introduce contributions for the NFV) and represent a direct (and rapidly increasing) burden on the fiscus, crowding out other social protection initiatives that are targeted at lower-income households.

Pension payments are received predominantly by wealthier households in urban areas: while 17.5% of households with at least one senior family member received a pension in the highest consumption quintile in urban areas, only 1.4% did so in the poorest quintile in 2014 (Figure 3.8). By contrast, pension benefit incidence was only about 3% in rural areas, with even lower coverage in the poorest rural quintile.

Table 3.1. **MoSVY budget breakdown (2016)**

Programmes	Spending, KHR (million)			Spending, USD (million)	% of MoSVY expenditure
	National	Provincial	Total		
NSSF-C	5 900	265 666	271 566	67.9	38.0
NFV	5 352	355 068	360 420	90.1	50.5
Emergency support to vulnerable groups	7 779	6 374	14 153	3.5	2.0
Child welfare	5 236	7 062	12 298	3.1	1.7
Disabled people	10 943	634	11 577	2.9	1.6
Elderly people	327	335	662	0.2	0.1
Others (institutional development, etc.)	205	43 044	43 249	10.8	6.1
Total MoSVY budget	**35 742**	**678 183**	**713 925**	**178.8**	**100**

Source: MoSVY (2016).

Figure 3.8. **Pension coverage is highest in urban areas**

Pension coverage by consumption quintile and region in Cambodia (2014)

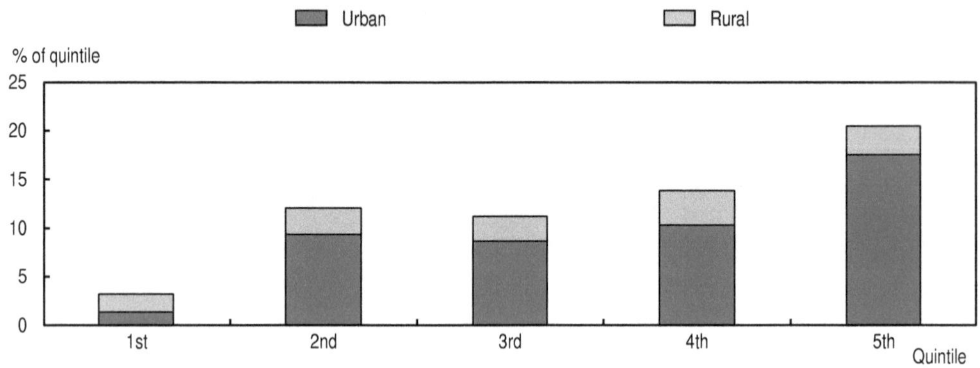

Note: The quintiles of household consumption in 2014 Cambodian riel (KHR) are defined according to the following cut-offs: 674 952 / 902 023 / 1 154 459 / 1 572 958 / 18 680 054.

Source: Authors' calculations based on NIS (2014), *Cambodia Socio-Economic Survey 2014*, available at *nada-nis.gov.kh/index.php/catalog/CSES*.

Between 2012 and 2016, spending on retirement benefits by the NSSF-C and the NFV increased approximately sixfold and fourfold respectively in nominal terms (Figure 3.9). This increase reflects growth in the number of civil servants, which has been reinforced by wage increases long considered necessary to improve conditions for state employees (World Bank, 2013). According to an actuarial analysis carried out by the ILO, civil service wages have increased by an average of 18% a year over the past ten years (ILO, forthcoming).

The minimum monthly salary for members of the NSSF-C and NFV is currently around USD 150. However, the RGC expects to raise it to around USD 250 as of 2018. Because replacement rates and minimum benefit levels are linked to current wages, salary increases automatically increase pension expenditures and liabilities.

The NSSF-C and the NFV are accruing long-term obligations that will constrain the RGC's spending decisions in the future even if contributions are enforced for one or even both arrangements. It is imperative that this debt be accurately quantified and recognised as part of the process of establishing a new pension system envisaged by the Social Protection Policy Framework (SPPF).

Figure 3.9. **Pension coverage and spending are rising**
NSSF-C and NFV beneficiaries and expenditure (2012-16)

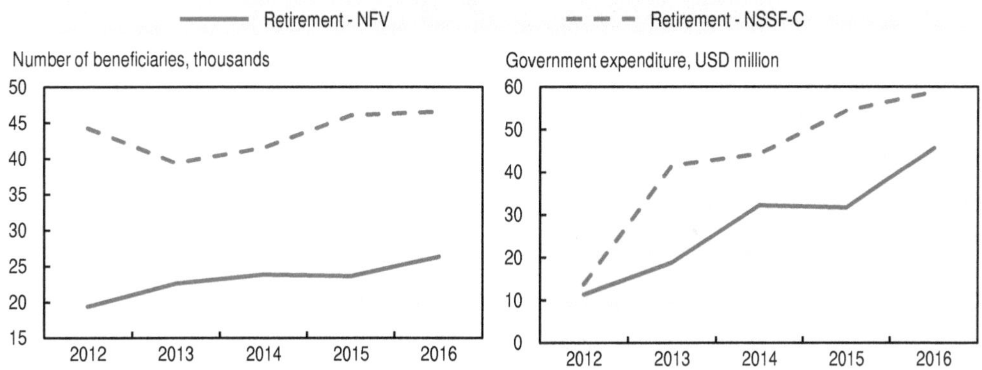

Source: Ministry of Economy and Finance (2016).

Cambodia's social protection spending is low by regional standards

According to the Asian Development Bank (ADB) Social Protection Index (SPI), only Indonesia spends a lower proportion of GDP on social protection than Cambodia at 0.5% of GDP, compared with Cambodia's 0.6% (Figure 3.10) (ADB, 2013). Viet Nam spent the most on social protection in Southeast Asia (SEA) in 2010 at over 5% of GDP. In 2009, Cambodia spent 0.2% of GDP on social insurance, 0.3% on social assistance and 0.1% on labour market programmes.

According to the ADB's SPI, Cambodia performed better than Lao PDR and Indonesia in average expenditure per beneficiary[5] but was much weaker than the rest of the comparison Association of Southeast Asian Nations (ASEAN) countries in terms of the percentage of GDP allocated to social protection (Figure 3.11). Cambodia's expenditures per intended beneficiary amounted to 2% of the poverty line (set at 25% of GDP per capita), compared with 9.5% for SEA as a whole.

Figure 3.10. **Social protection expenditure in Cambodia is among the lowest in the region**

Social protection expenditure in SEA, % of GDP (2008-10)

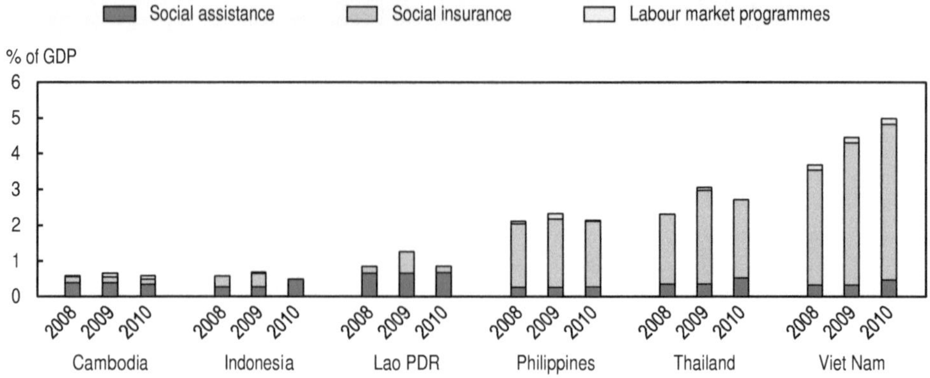

Note: Lao PDR = Lao People's Democratic Republic.

Source: ADB (2013), *Social Protection Index* (database), *hdl.handle.net/11540/79*, accessed September 2016.

Figure 3.11. **Cambodia's depth and breadth of social protection are low by regional standards**

Depth and breadth of social protection in SEA, ADB SPI score (2013)

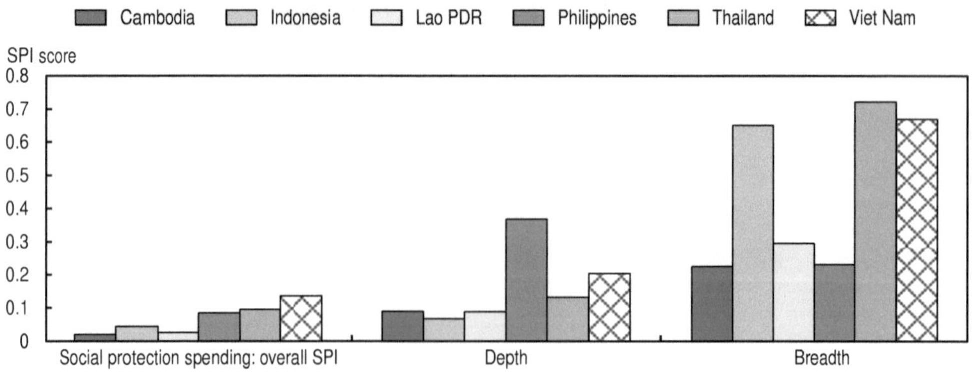

Note: In the Social Protection Index, *depth* refers to the ratio of total expenditures to total beneficiaries (normalised by the value of the relative poverty line), while *breadth* refers to the ratio of total beneficiaries to the total reference population. Depth can thus be interpreted as the average expenditure per actual beneficiary as a percentage of poverty line expenditures.

Source: ADB (2013), *Social Protection Index* (database), *hdl.handle.net/11540/79*, accessed September 2016.

Taxes and transfers are failing to reduce poverty

Countries are increasingly assessing the coherence of fiscal and social policies to ensure complementarity. Revenue and expenditure measures are mutually reinforcing; people pay the taxes that fund public services and social protection transfers. Considering only the revenue or expenditure side of the fiscal framework when analysing government efforts to reduce poverty and inequality provides only a partial picture (Bastagli, 2015).

In 2015, value added tax (VAT) on imported goods accounted for 2.0% of Cambodia's gross domestic product (GDP), VAT on domestic goods accounted for 1.2% of GDP, and excise duties on imported and domestic goods accounted for 2.2% of GDP. Payroll taxes have been on an overall upward trajectory, from 0.3% of GDP in 2010 to 0.6% in 2014 and 0.4% in 2015. The tax on company profits was a much more important source of revenue at 1.9% of GDP. Those revenues are expected to increase from 2016 onwards as a result of a push for companies to register on the "real" rather than "estimated" tax regime.

Modelling based on 2014 CSES data suggests that the quantum of tax paid rises with consumption; so too does the average tax rate (Figure 3.12). The average tax rate is notably lower for the poorest decile. It jumps for the second decile and thereafter increases relatively mildly until the seventh decile, at which it levels off until the tenth. The increase in both quantum of tax and tax rate for the tenth decile reflects both increased consumption at the top end of the distribution and the fact that only the very top earners are likely to pay the salary tax.[6]

Figure 3.12. **Cambodia's tax system is progressive**

Tax quantum and average tax rate by consumption decile per capita in Cambodia (2014)

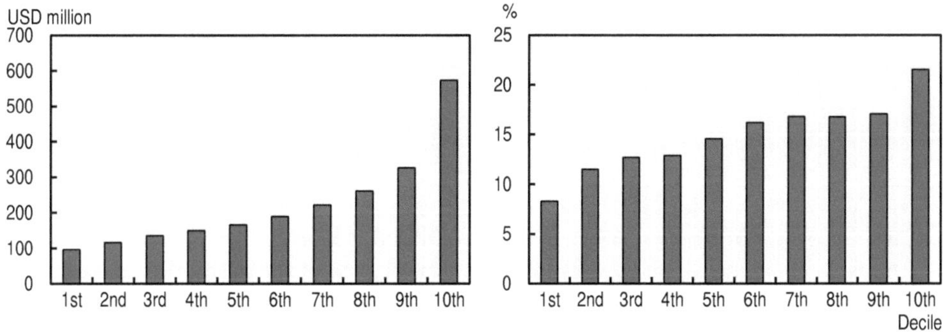

Note: The deciles of household consumption per capita in 2014 Cambodian riel (KHR) are defined according to the following cut-offs: 131 675/ 157 611 / 181 599 / 203 509 / 228 697 / 258 686 / 294 930 / 352 555 / 456 316.

Source: Authors' calculations based on NIS (2014), *Cambodia Socio-Economic Survey 2014.*

Figure 3.13 shows the net effect of taxes and transfers on the income distribution using counterfactual analysis. It models four scenarios. The baseline scenario models the status quo, i.e. current household consumption after the receipt of social protection benefits and payment of taxes. The first counterfactual scenario models household consumption in the absence of public transfers. The second counterfactual scenario models household consumption in the absence of taxes. The third counterfactual scenario models household consumption after subtracting both transfers and taxes.

The model highlights two important trends. First, inequality (as evident from the disparity in consumption levels across the distribution) is lower after taxes but the receipt of transfers plays a minimal role in equalising consumption levels because the coverage and level of benefits is low. Second, all groups along the income distribution, including the poorest, would have higher levels of consumption in the absence of taxes, with or without transfers.

Figure 3.13. **Taxes and transfers are failing to reduce poverty**

Mean annual per capita consumption by decile in Cambodia, in USD: baseline and counterfactual scenarios (2014)

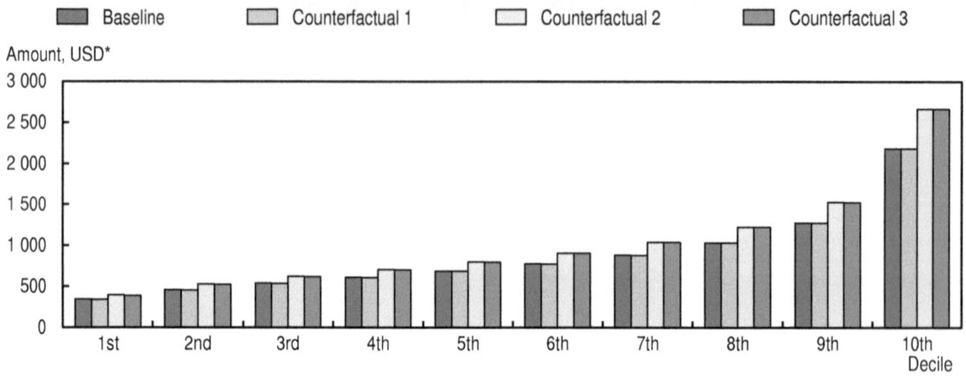

Notes: * USD = United States dollar.
Baseline (status quo) = transfers and taxes; counterfactual 1 = taxes, no transfers; counterfactual 2 = transfers, no taxes; counterfactual 3 = no transfers, no taxes.The deciles of household consumption per capita in 2014 Cambodian riel (KHR) are defined according to the following cut-offs: 131 675/ 157 611 / 181 599 / 203 509 / 228 697 / 258 686 / 294 930 / 352 555 / 456 316.

Source: Authors' calculations based on NIS (2014), *Cambodia Socio-Economic Survey 2014.*

The average total tax burden for poor households is 14.9% of the average total consumption and 67.8% of the national poverty line. For the many households close to the poverty line, taxation can mean the difference between being above or below the threshold. Calculations based on the 2014 CSES show that taxation pushes about 5.1% of the population (166 322 households or 774 389 individuals) into poverty.

The impact of social protection transfers in alleviating poverty is modest due to their low coverage and benefit levels. Based on microsimulations of existing social protection programmes, 0.6% of the population (19 567 households or 91 105 individuals) who have post-tax per capita consumption above the poverty line would be poor without these transfers. Figure 3.14 shows estimates for the headcount poverty rate in the absence of transfers and taxes; it indicates that, while progressive, the fiscal framework's net impact is impoverishing.

These calculations confirm the importance of assessing the combined effect of taxes and transfers. If the SPPF is to achieve the poverty reduction objectives, transfer amounts will have to increase to offset the impact of taxation on the poor. This is especially the case should official development assistance be declining (as discussed in Chapter 4). Thinking ahead to the implementation of the SPPF, it will be important to assess the impact of different financing strategies, especially on poor and vulnerable households.

Figure 3.14. **Transfers are not sufficient to offset the impact of taxes**

Poverty headcount rate according to taxes and transfers in Cambodia: baseline and counterfactual scenarios (2014)

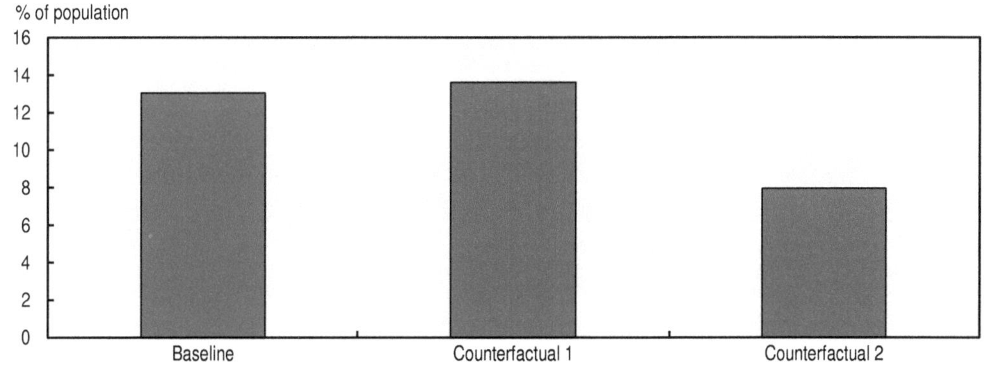

Notes: Baseline (status quo) = transfers and taxes; counterfactual 1 = taxes, no transfers; counterfactual 2 = transfers, no taxes.

Source: Authors' calculations based on NIS (2014), *Cambodia Socio-Economic Survey 2014.*

Notes

1. The first Kanta Bopha paediatric hospital was established in 1992 and since they have grown to a network of hospitals which are funded mainly through private donations and support from the Swiss Agency for Development and Cooperation.
2. According to the World Health Organization's definition of catastrophic health expenditure.
3. The social sector contains the Ministries of Information; Health; Education, Youth, and Sport; Culture and Fine Arts; Environment; Social and Veteran Affairs and Youth Rehabilitation; Cults and Religion; Women Affairs; and Labour and Vocational Training.
4. The economic sector comprises the Ministries of Agriculture, Forestry and Fisheries; Rural Development; Public Works and Transport; and Water Resources and Meteorology.
5. Divided by the national poverty line to adjust for differences in GDP per capita (ADB, 2013).
6. These estimates are based on microsimulation of seven major taxes, including taxes on profit, salaries, property, VAT, excise tax, and tax on petroleum imports and other import duties.

References

ADB (2013), *The Social Protection Index Assessing Results for Asia and the Pacific*, Asian Development Bank, Manila, *www.adb.org/sites/default/files/publication/30293/social-protection-index.pdf*.

Bastagli, F. (2015), "Bringing taxation into social protection analysis and planning", *ODI Working Paper*, No. 421, The Overseas Development Institute, London, *odi.org/publications/9671-bringing-taxation-social-protection-analysis-and-planning-working-paper*.

Flores, G. et al. (2013), "Financial protection of patients through compensation of providers: The impact of health equity funds in Cambodia", *Journal of Health Economics*, Vol. 32, Issue 6, pp. 1180-1193, *http://dx.doi.org/10.1016/j.jhealeco.2013.09.012*.

ILO (forthcoming), *Actuarial valuation of the National Social Security Fund for the Civil Servants and actuarial study on the implementation of a new pension scheme in the private sector*, International Labour Organization, Geneva.

Levine, D. et al. (2010), *Assessing the Effects of Health Insurance: The SKY Micro-Insurance Program in Rural Cambodia*, Impact Analyses Series, No. 4, Agence française de développement, Paris, *librairie.afd.fr/en/assessing-the-effects-of-health-insurance-the-sky-microinsurance-program-in-rural-cambodia/*.

NIS (2014), *Cambodia Socio-Economic Survey 2014*, National Institute of Statistics, Ministry of Planning, Royal Government of Cambodia, Phnom Penh.

NIS (2009), *Cambodia Socio-Economic Survey 2009, Household Survey 2009*, National Institute of Statistics, Ministry of Planning, Royal Government of Cambodia, Phnom Penh.

NIS (2004), *Cambodia Socio-Economic Survey 2004, Household Survey 2004*, National Institute of Statistics, Ministry of Planning, Royal Government of Cambodia, Phnom Penh.

World Bank (2013), *Public service pay in Cambodia: the challenges of salary reform*, World Bank, Washington, DC, *documents.worldbank.org/curated/en/913481468214829704/Public-service-pay-in-Cambodia-the-challenges-of-salary-reform*.

Chapter 4

Systematising social protection in Cambodia

This chapter proposes a scaling-up of social assistance and a consolidation of social insurance arrangements in line with Cambodia's 2017 Social Protection Policy Framework (SPPF). While domestic resource mobilisation policies are proving highly successful, the sustainable implementation of the SPPF will require a financing strategy. Finally, this chapter recommends measures to improve coherence across the social protection system and the expansion of tools for implementing, monitoring and evaluating social protection provision.

This chapter proposes policies to support the Royal Government of Cambodia's plans for establishing of a social protection system. These recommendations are based on the evidence presented in the first three chapters of the review and are aligned to the policies and priorities outlined by the Social Protection Policy Framework (SPPF) published in 2017.

Chapter 1 identifies considerable livelihoods challenges lie ahead for Cambodia in spite of its impressive progress in reducing poverty and developing its economy. The decline in poverty is slowing and broader measures of deprivation have not fallen as far as monetary policy. Children are especially at risk: malnutrition among children under five years old is a problem across all income groups, while the low proportion of children who finish secondary school and the large number of children who are in the labour market are also a major concern. Informal employment is growing rapidly and many workers are in low-paid or vulnerable employment. Climate change is emerging as a major threat to homes and livelihoods and Cambodia's demographics will become less favourable over time.

As Chapter 2 recognises, Cambodia has the building blocks for a social protection system that can respond to these challenges. A legal framework is in place, the SPPF is the second policy document for the sector as a whole and numerous schemes exist for each one of the system's three pillars – social assistance, social insurance and labour market programmes. Health Equity Funds are leading the way towards Universal Health Coverage in Cambodia, with the poorest households among the first to benefit. The IDPoor targeting system is both transparent and effective at identifying those most at need. However, not all risks are covered by existing social protection instruments and Cambodia's rapidly growing urban areas are poorly served by anti-poverty schemes.

Moreover, as Chapter 3 shows, existing social protection schemes are limited in terms of coverage and benefit levels; as a result, they have little impact on poverty. Although Cambodia's public expenditure on social protection is increasing, its spending remains low by regional standards and the vast majority of these resources are used to finance pension benefits paid to retired civil servants and military veterans through arrangements that are still tax-financed rather than contributory. As a result, social spending is neither pro-poor nor sufficient to offset the impact of taxes on household consumption among poor and vulnerable households, with the overall effect that the fiscal system exacerbates poverty.

This chapter identifies specific interventions that can underpin the development of Cambodia's social protection system, as envisaged by the SPPF. These proposed interventions will operate at a policy, programme or administrative level and will adopt a four-pillar approach, based on creating, expanding, reforming and sustaining the components of a new social protection system within a single, coherent and overarching framework.

Achieve a strategic and systematic expansion of social assistance

Chapter 1 indicated various factors which will not only limit further gains in reducing poverty but will also jeopardise the gains that have been achieved. It shows that a significant proportion of the poor are chronic poor, meaning that they have not benefited from the rapid growth of Cambodia's economy in recent years and are not likely to do so in the future unless the nature of this growth changes. At the same time, the characteristics and location of poverty are evolving and there is frequent movement in and out of poverty. It is also important to note that overall living standards have not improved as fast as incomes: the multi-dimensional poverty rate is far higher than income poverty.

This section proposes different policy options for enhancing the impact of social assistance. It does not examine the implementation issues associated with these proposals, since these form the basis of a separate analysis of the capacity to implement the SPPF's social assistance recommendations, as carried out by the European Union Social Protection Systems Programme (Box 4.1).

Scaling up social assistance with a focus on the young and very young

Existing social assistance programmes – including programmes implemented by the RGC and development partners respectively – address the needs outlined in Chapter 1 but are highly fragmented and do not operate at sufficient scale to address these problems at a national level. Nor are they linked to other social protection programmes.

There is a clear case for these programmes to be scaled up, not only to improve the living conditions of children but also to address broader concerns around the lack of skills among the workforce and long-term issues around competiveness. The SPPF maintains the current emphasis on programmes that support human development. In a context where caregiving responsibilities are an important contributor to poverty, scholarship programmes promote school attendance by offsetting the direct and indirect costs of educating children.

However, these schemes only operate for certain grades, do not operate country-wide, are implemented by different agencies (domestic and international) and are reliant (in part) on financial support from development partners, which raises doubts as to their sustainability and capacity to expand.

Moreover, there is a clear case for starting social protection interventions earlier, as demonstrated by the high levels of malnutrition among children under five years old. This review strongly supports the SPPF's commitment to the gradual implementation of a nutrition promotion programme for children and pregnant women at a national level which is complemented by a policy for free counselling and medical check-ups for pregnant women. Given that malnutrition is a problem that affects a large proportion of children across the income distribution, consideration should be given to making this a universal programme.

There is a clear investment case for introducing a programme for children and pregnant women. Early childhood interventions not only strengthen cognitive development at an age when such programmes yield the greatest long-term gains (Heckman, 2008), but also reinforce the impact of scholarships and school feeding programmes when children are ready for school.

The Identification of Poor Households Programme (IDPoor) database (discussed in greater detail below) could provide a mechanism for ensuring that beneficiaries of a programme aimed at one stage of the lifecycle are automatically enrolled in a social protection programme later in life, including labour-market initiatives beyond education. In practice, existing social protection schemes do not operate at sufficient scale to ensure this continuity of coverage, with the possible exception of the Health Equity Funds (HEF).

Shifting from emergency response to developmental programmes

The need for better co-ordination between emergency response measures and other social assistance programmes (as proposed by the SPPF) is an important aspect of systematisation. It is important that the national disaster management strategy identify areas that are regular recipients of emergency assistance so that permanent social protection programmes be established in these areas. This shift will not only improve the speed at which communities in these areas who are affected by a natural disaster can be reached but will also allow these communities to increase their resilience *ex ante*, for example by climate-proofing their land and infrastructure or diversifying their activities. In so doing, social protection not only safeguards livelihoods but, at an aggregate level, promotes greater long-term productivity in the agricultural sector.

Placing greater emphasis on social assistance programmes aimed at improving human development rather than those that provide temporary support (typically food aid) will also yield longer-term benefits for recipients. However, better aligning the emergency response with human development social assistance programmes faces an institutional constraint, namely the fact that the Ministry of Economy and Finance (MoEF) directly manages the budget for emergency response. Such an arrangement reflects the challenge that line ministries experience in budgeting for national disasters, whose impact, location and duration is impossible to know in advance. Targeting especially at-risk areas with conventional social assistance programmes is a useful means of reducing the proportion of the emergency relief budget for which the MoEF is responsible.

Better integrating public works programmes to social protection and development plans

Public works programmes (PWPs) have been an important poverty-reduction instrument in Cambodia since 1993, with the result that the country has generated significant experience and expertise in implementing such programmes. However, PWPs have relied overwhelmingly on support from the World Food Programme and the Asian Development Bank and do not feature in the SPPF. This exclusion likely reflects two factors: the low rate of unemployment and the fact that PWPs are costly relative to other interventions. However, PWPs can adapt from being primarily poverty-alleviation instruments to interventions which simultaneously develop economic assets and provide training and work experience to low-skilled workers. Although this shift would increase the cost of such programmes, it would also greatly increase their broader economic benefits.

As an example of how this might work, Cambodia suffers from severe infrastructure deficits, which are particularly pronounced in rural areas and thus a major constraint on the competitiveness of the agricultural sector. PWPs can help not only meet these infrastructure needs (for example by building rural roads and improving irrigation) but can also maintain new infrastructure assets and thus greatly increase their lifespan. At the same time, the programmes can target specific groups at risk of under-employment or unproductive work (such as youth) and emphasise the training provided to participants. In so doing they can increase social protection among the vulnerable labour force, which is currently reliant on technical vocational education and training (TVET) (whose coverage is limited).

This might also be a means of expanding access to social protection into urban areas, which are currently underserved in this regard – a situation that cannot be sustained in a context of rapid urbanisation and thus an increase in the absolute number of urban poor. Expanding and adapting the IDPoor targeting mechanism (as mentioned below) to urban contexts is an important means of understanding the characteristics and needs of the urban poor and vulnerable. This knowledge should be used to ensure that the social protection programmes implemented in urban areas do not simply mimic the design of rural interventions.

Box 4.1. **Developing the capacity to expand social assistance**

The European Union Social Protection Systems Programme (EU-SPS) has analysed the RGC's capacity to implement the SPPF objectives related to social assistance (THL, forthcoming). This research ran in parallel to this review and its findings are an essential complement.

This report reviews the governance and implementation landscape of the current social assistance system and relates this to broader public sector reforms, most notably the decentralisation process. It also identifies the key actors involved in the co-ordination and implementation of social assistance programmes at central and subnational levels and assesses their capacity to enact reforms proposed by the SPPF. Capacity in this case refers to institutions' formal mandate as well as the scope and effectiveness of their administrative structures.

The study suggests a number of guiding principles on the future governance structure for the social assistance schemes, the development of appropriate capacity to implement the system envisaged by the SPPF and the need for sequencing reforms to overcome current capacity constraints. It also analyses appropriate structures for the national-level co-ordination of social assistance, the co-ordination of implementation and the implementation activities themselves.

The SPPF requires a long-term financing plan

Scaling up social assistance in the ways that are outlined above would allow it to make a significant impact in reducing poverty. However, it would also require a significant increase in the resources allocated to social protection, which would have to be sustained over a prolonged period. The SPPF proposes a gradual increase to social assistance that should not represent an unmanageable burden on public finances. The macroeconomic situation is favourable to such a scaling up: the RGC has greater fiscal resources at its disposal to increase the scope of social protection thanks to progress in increasing revenue generation at an even faster rate than that at which the economy has grown.

However, as Chapter 3 shows, social protection spending is low by regional standards and tax-funded pension payments to retired civil servants and military veterans are eliminating any fiscal space that might be opening up for social protection. A detailed plan for sustainably financing the expansion of social protection is an important complement to the SPPF.

Tax revenues as a proportion of gross domestic product (GDP) have risen from 9.7% in 2009 to an estimated 14.3% of GDP in 2015 (Figure 4.1) – a performance driven by the RGC's success in enhancing tax compliance, particularly with regard to encouraging businesses to register formally. This increase has helped the government to consolidate public finances by reducing the fiscal deficit rather than increase spending, in keeping with a counter-cyclical approach to public spending.

Figure 4.1. **Tax revenues have grown as a share of GDP**
Government revenue in Cambodia (2009-15)

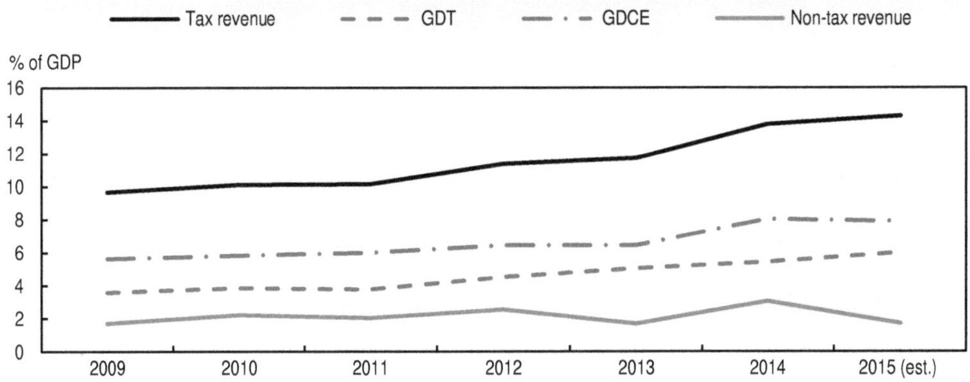

Note: GDT refers to the General Department of Taxation, which is responsible for domestic revenues, while GDCE refers to the General Department of Customs and Excise, whose mandate covers trade-related revenues. Values for 2015 are estimated.
Source: Ministry of Economy and Finance (2016).

Figure 4.2 shows the revenues generated by different tax instruments from 2010 to 2015. Indirect and trade taxes provide the bulk of trade revenues but there is evidence of an upwards trend in receipts from taxes on profits and salaries (Cambodia doesn't have a personal income tax per se). This shift towards more progressive tax instruments complements the proposed increase in social protection spending both in terms of reducing poverty and improving the distributional impact of the fiscal framework.

These increases in revenues have coincided with stable spending levels. As shown in Figure 4.3, total spending in 2015 was 21% of GDP, which is the same level as in 2009 (though it did increase in the intervening years). The combined effect of increased revenues and steady spending has been to reduce the fiscal deficit from 9.5% of GDP in 2009 to 4.5% of GDP in 2015. At the same time, the debt level remains low (at 33% of GDP). However, wage increases for civil servants are expected to increase expenditure from 2016 onwards and are likely to increase the fiscal deficit.

While the SPPF identifies the financing challenges that confront different social insurance instruments, it does not contain a long-term financing strategy for expanding the social protection system as a whole. Given that the SPPF recommends the introduction and scaling up of a number of different programmes, it is important to understand the overall financing requirement and devise an implementation strategy that reflects the priorities for the sector through a costed action plan, containing different options for scaling up according to different future scenarios (for example, related to economic growth).

Figure 4.2. **The balance between tax instruments is evolving**

Tax instrument revenue in Cambodia (2010-15)

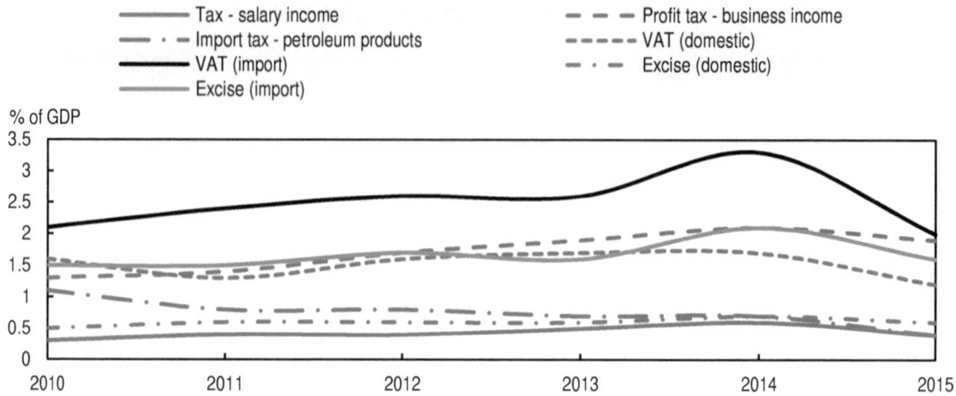

Source: Ministry of Economy and Finance (2016).

Figure 4.3. **The fiscal balance has improved**

Revenues, expenditure and fiscal deficit in Cambodia (2009-17)

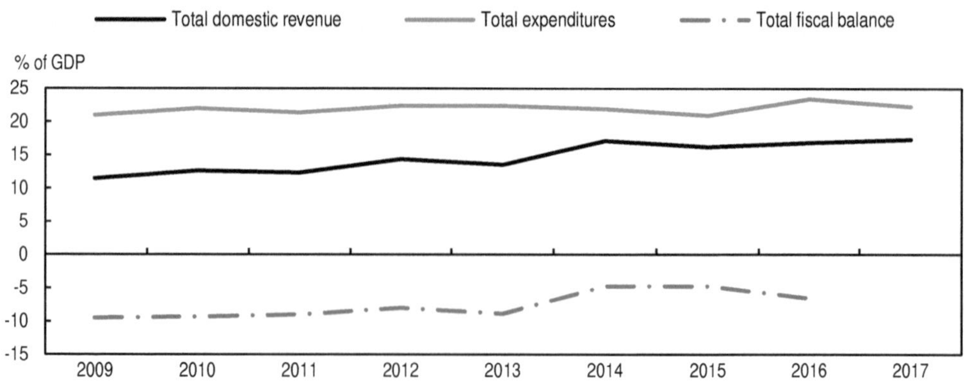

Source: Ministry of Economy and Finance (2016).

It is also necessary to forecast how the RGC's resource envelope is likely to grow over time and how much of the spending envelope is likely to be allocated to social protection. Integrating social protection within the RGC's broader development plans is crucial in this regard. Moreover, it is also essential to understand the impact of the tax system in terms of both redistribution and the reduction in consumption: increasing taxes to finance social protection risks exacerbating poverty if poor individuals are net payers to the fiscus rather than net beneficiaries.

Box 4.2. **The level and type of development assistance is changing**

Development partners have played a major role in funding social protection programmes in Cambodia. The World Food Programme, Asian Development Bank, United Nations Children's Fund (UNICEF), Deutsche Gesellschaft für Internationale Zusammenarbeit (GIZ), European Union (EU) and others fund the pillars of Cambodia's social protection system: scholarships, TVET and HEF. They also finance relatively small-scale pilots, providing for antenatal and early childhood benefits and home-grown school feeding programmes.

However, Cambodia's graduation to lower-middle income status is likely to change the dynamics. Already, the level of official development assistance (ODA) is not keeping up with growth in the economy, falling from 4.1% of GDP in 2010 to 1.9% of GDP in 2015 (National Bank of Cambodia, 2016). Moreover, the composition of Cambodia's ODA is changing (Figure 4.4). Data from the OECD Development Assistance Committee shows concessional lending for economic and infrastructure services has grown strongly and now accounts for the majority of ODA, while assistance for social infrastructure and services in 2015 was at approximately the same level in absolute terms as in 2010 and has thus fallen significantly as a proportion of GDP.

This change in the structure of ODA is typical as countries' income level rises. A corollary of this change is that the terms of assistance become less favourable for the government, since the investments supported by ODA are expected to generate an economic return.

Figure 4.4. **The composition of ODA to Cambodia is changing**

Official development assistance to Cambodia by sector (2007-15)

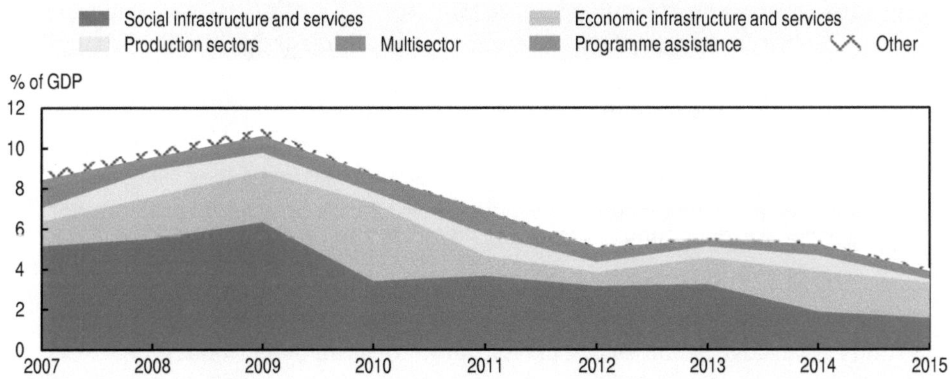

Note: All numbers indexed to 2015. "Other" includes unallocated funds, action relating to debt and humanitarian aid.

Source: OECD (2017), OECD.Stat (database), *stats.oecd.org*.

Integrating social insurance arrangements for efficiency and equity

Cambodia's social insurance programmes are in their infancy and, at present, are highly fragmented. Given that the population will start to age rapidly within the next 30 years (as discussed in Chapter 1), it is important that the SPPF's recommendations for developing social insurance are acted upon quickly while preserving the overall objective of deepening systematisation.

As Chapter 2 shows, access to social security relies on individuals working in the formal sector even though informal employment is increasing rapidly and accounts for the majority of the workforce. Moreover, the extent and type of coverage depends on whether employees are in the private or public sector: public sector workers have access to pension arrangements but not yet health insurance, while private-sector workers do not have access to a pension arrangement but are covered by employment injury insurance and health insurance through the National Social Security Fund.

This fragmentation is reflected in the institutional structure for social insurance. Three principal arrangements exist, each established by different legislation with a separate governance structure: the National Social Security Fund (NSSF), the National Social Security Fund for Civil Servants (NSSF-C) and the National Fund for Veterans (NFV). Financing arrangements also differ between the three. The NSSF and NSSF-C are intended to be contributory arrangements while the NFV is run on a non-contributory basis, meaning pension payments are financed by general tax revenues. In reality, the NSSF-C is also non-contributory: the 2011 decree stipulating a total contribution rate of 24% of a civil servant's salary has yet to be implemented.

As a result, pension payments for retired civil servants are financed through general taxation via the budget of the Ministry of Social Affairs, Veterans and Youth Rehabilitation (MoSVY). It accounts for a large (and rapidly growing) proportion of spending by the MoSVY. Moreover, the government balance sheet does not reflect the long-term liability that is being generated by the NSSF-C through the commitment to provide a pension to current civil servants when they retire. This implicit debt is growing as civil service wages increase. In actuarial terms, this arrangement is insolvent for as long as this debt is not acknowledged and matched.

Notwithstanding the urgency of enforcing contribution to the NSSF-C (the NFV arrangement is expected to remain non-contributory) and recognising both funds' respective liabilities, the present situation is an opportunity for the RGC to devise an integrated framework for social insurance. This framework would ideally be based on a single pension arrangement (providing a comprehensive range of benefits) for all formal-sector workers. A similar arrangement for health insurance would also be optimal, as is discussed below.

Consistent with this, the RGC is currently considering a general pension scheme, in which private-sector workers and new civil servants will be enrolled. Under this dispensation, the NSSF-C would be closed to new members and its debt would be ring-fenced so that it is not transferred to the private sector. The NSSF-C would still become a contributory scheme but would slowly wind down.

From a systematic perspective, a single statutory pension arrangement provides numerous advantages at an institutional, administrative and policy level. Integrating mandatory pension arrangements for private-sector and new public-sector workers into a single statutory scheme would maximise potential economies of scale in terms of administration and governance. It would also guarantee fairness across these arrangements and minimise any distortions of the labour market associated with individuals opting to work in one sector due to better social security arrangements (at a given salary level).

The SPPF envisages that the mandatory pension system will comprise public and private sector arrangements which will share information systems and will "be consistent" with each other to ensure portability of benefits (and thus facilitate staff movement between the public and private sectors). However, there is a strong case for merging the public and private sector arrangements. It has not yet been decided whether the public and private sector funds will be designed as funded or unfunded arrangements but in either case the rationale for discrete arrangements is weak if the intention is to ensure consistency between the two.

If a funded defined contribution arrangement is selected for both arrangements, the system is better understood as one comprising individual accounts for each contributor rather than stand-alone funds for the public and private sectors. Achieving consistency in such a context is straightforward: the contribution rate, investment rules, governance arrangements and pay-out mechanisms should be the same for workers in the public and private sectors. If an unfunded arrangement (either defined benefit or defined contribution) is selected, ensuring consistency between discrete public- and private-sector arrangements would be much harder because the risk pools are different.

For example, in most countries the contribution density and risk profile differ between public and private sector workers (often in favour of the former). While it might be possible to offer the same level of benefits to members of these different arrangements under such circumstances, other parameters would have to differ in order to ensure they are both sustainable, such as the contribution rate or retirement age. This undermines consistency between the two arrangements, complicates portability and raises major equity concerns. This issue would fall away if a general pension scheme is established.

A detailed discussion of the appropriate design for the new pension system is beyond the scope of this paper. In broad terms, the shallowness of Cambodia's financial markets is a major obstacle to generating the investment returns on which funded arrangements depend. The country's demographics are supportive of a pay-as-you-go arrangement, which (if a defined benefit design is chosen) can guarantee an adequate level of benefits. However, it is important that the system does not make excessive promises to today's workforce that will impose an unfair or unmanageable burden on future generations in the form of higher contribution rates to finance pension payments. Whichever system is chosen, it is essential that the legacy costs of the current system (the non-contributory NSSF-C and NFV arrangements) are properly accounted for.

Box 4.3. **Placing the garment sector at the heart of the social protection system**

According to the International Labour Organization, registered garment and footwear factories employed 610 000 workers in 2016, which is roughly a third of the total enterprise workforce (as calculated by the 2011 Enterprise Survey) (ILO, 2017; NIS and MoP, 2011). The total annual salary bill for the sector was USD 1.4 billion in 2016. The RGC's strategy for including these workers within tax and social security arrangements will have major implications for public finances and the viability of social security arrangements in the future.

The RGC has focused on garment and footwear factories for implementing both the Employment Injury Insurance (EII) and the social health insurance (SHI), which has led to relatively quick increases in coverage of both arrangements through the NSSF. This success indicates that it would also be relatively straightforward administratively to implement a pension scheme for these workers.

However, the same workers are deliberately excluded from paying tax: the minimum salary tax threshold of USD 250 per month in 2016 was well above the minimum wage (USD 140 per month) and the average salary in the sector (USD 222 per month). Fringe benefits are also exempt from taxation.

The exclusion of garment workers from the tax system lowers the cost of employment, which is an important aspect of Cambodia's export competitiveness. However, it also imposes a constraint on domestic resource mobilisation and could have implications for the distributional impact of the tax system if it requires additional resources to be generated from indirect taxes rather than the graduated (and thus progressive) salary tax.

Moreover, it should be noted that the rate of pension contributions (when these are introduced) is likely to be considerably higher than the 5% marginal income tax rate for workers in the lower band (which has an upper threshold of USD 375 in 2016). Such contributions, whether made by the employer or employee, have a similar impact on the cost of employment as taxes on income.

It is necessary to understand the likely interaction between the mandatory arrangements and an eventual social pension. The value of the social pension benefit should be set at a level which protects recipients from poverty but which is not sufficiently high to deter participation in the mandatory scheme. This would especially important in the case of the voluntary fund for informal workers currently envisaged by the SPPF. If the value of the contributory pension is not significantly higher than that of the social pension then potential contributors to the former will have no reason to enrol and the cost of protecting them from poverty in old age will fall predominantly on the state – specifically, the employers and employees of the day who pay their taxes. Given the current level of social benefits, however, this problem is unlikely to arise.

The SPPF envisages separate processes for reforming or establishing the civil service pension scheme, the private-sector pension scheme, a voluntary fund for higher earners, a fund for informal workers and the social pension. To ensure coherence at an institutional and policy level across the retirement space, the process for designing different components of the retirement landscape needs to happen at once and include all role players, including social partners. This might prolong the process but retirement systems have a lifespan and an impact (for better or worse) that cross multiple generations; it is worth tolerating delays in the short term to design a system that is fair and sustainable in the long term.

Universal health coverage can be achieved through greater systematisation

The SPPF traces an ambitious path to universal health coverage (UHC) for Cambodia, building on existing and recently developed health financing and health system innovations. HEF have improved financial access to health services, especially for the poorest 20% of the population. The recently approved Health Equity and Quality Improvement project, funded by donors and the RGC, will further strengthen the operational environment of HEF. At the same time, recent progress in rolling out social health insurance through the NSSF has increased coverage among formal sector workers and built up capacity required to manage a health insurance mechanism.

Alongside the demand-side reforms, improving the supply of health services is crucial. Here, the RGC can build on the service delivery grants (SDGs) and the monitoring and evaluation mechanisms built into them - although more evidence is still needed on the effectiveness and efficiency of the SDG model. The challenge of upgrading public health service provision is noted by the SPPF and is seen as a necessary step in increasing effective coverage. The accreditation body envisaged by the SPPF, which will ensure quality in both public and private health facilities, is also an important element of the overall UHC strategy.

A systemic approach to achieving UHC will be developed on three fronts:

- Further extending the formal sector coverage (coverage of all private sector formal salaried workers and rolling out the health insurance system to civil servants)
- Further expanding population and service coverage through HEF as a targeted measure for the poor and near poor and consolidating financing for HEF
- Reaching the "missing middle" – the "non-poor" informal sector workers – through a comprehensive approach as discussed below.

While many countries are following this path to UHC, there are many pitfalls to avoid. One of the major challenges lies in reaching the "missing middle", often defined as "non-poor" informal-sector workers who are expected to enrol through direct contributions. It has been shown in many countries, including Cambodia in the case of community-based health insurance (CBHI), that voluntary (or de facto voluntary) contributory health insurance mechanisms tend to fail in encouraging enrolment. They often struggle with adverse selection; in Indonesia, for example, the claims ratio for the voluntary, non-poor informal sector is around 600%, indicating that enrolment attracts mainly high-risk (and therefore relatively costly) individuals (Tandon et al., 2016).

In the context of Cambodia, where 55% of the population is either poor or vulnerable and informal employment predominates, the level of contributions for non-salaried workers will confront challenges related to affordability and regularity. At the same time, the non-poor informal sector with capacity to pay into a contributory system is a relatively small cohort; a separate pool designed for this population segment will face great challenges with regard to sufficiency of revenues and adverse selection.

There are three principal mechanisms for reaching the "missing middle":

- Extension of health coverage through formalisation policies.

Formalisation of the workforce is a key means of ensuring the enhancement and financial sustainability of health coverage. Formalisation will increase coverage by (gradually) squeezing out the "missing middle". As the workforce formalises, the effect of more people being under a clear mandate to enrol in social protection schemes and the new revenue streams this entails, will increase health coverage and ensure its sustainable funding.

- Creating cross-subsidies between different population groups.

The SPPF establishes principles for moving towards a single health insurance operator. However, there is still some uncertainty about the extent of cross-subsidisation between the different schemes with the single operator as well as if and how much of the funds will be pooled together. Pooling funds together from different revenue streams would allow cross-subsidies between population groups and would open options to enrol the vulnerable through contribution subsidies.

- Higher funding through budget transfers.

The size of the poor and vulnerable population means that inclusion under any coverage mechanism cannot rely on large, direct contributions from individuals. Increasing coverage to the "missing middle" will require their contributions to be subsidised in some way. While this can, to some extent, be achieved through cross-subsidies from contributions of formal sector workers, it will also require matching contributions from the government, financed by general tax revenues. The envisaged expansion of HEF already relies on public funding.

In addition to the extension of coverage, focus needs to be given to the health benefit package, which will determine the "depth" of coverage. The SPPF proposes to study the feasibility of a unified package for all social health insurance schemes. Currently there are several packages for different schemes; unifying these packages and making informed decisions on inclusion and exclusion of services and medicine based on cost-effectiveness and equity criteria is essential for establishing clear entitlements.

Chile, for example, has established a guaranteed package of services based on clear guidelines related to both cost-effectiveness and equity criteria. This package, part of the AUGE reform, is accompanied by guaranteed access to services and guaranteed minimum waiting times (Missoni and Solimano, 2010). However, in the Cambodian context, the supply-side gaps are still important; effective coverage, especially in rural areas, will not be defined by the benefit package but by the availability and quality of health services. The upgrading of health service provision is thus a necessary condition for moving towards UHC.

A well-designed provider-payment mechanism and purchasing strategy are also necessary to ensure that incentives for providers are aligned with the objectives behind the UHC policy and that resources are used efficiently. In Cambodia, HEF and the service delivery grants have already laid the ground for purchasing mechanisms that focus on incentivising efficiency and improved quality. This needs to be further developed and brought to a system-wide level. It is also important to note that the SPPF emphasises the need to include private-sector service providers in the delivery of the package. This will be crucial: as Chapter 2 shows, private health providers are the primary choice for individuals seeking healthcare even if they are covered by HEF. The provider payment design will thus need to incentivise the engagement of the private sector.

Finally, institutional integration and setting up an overarching governance system for health coverage are both essential. The health sector will need to work towards institutional integration of the different insurance mechanisms in creating a single operator as intended by the SPPF. Managing this transition will not happen in isolation; it needs to be aligned with the broader social insurance integration discussed above. In practice, this would require that the single operator for the integrated health insurance system has a clear mandate and governance structure which are defined as part of the broader integration of social insurance and social protection processes to avoid overlaps and ambiguities.

Building a social protection information system based on IDPoor and CSES

Cambodia's arrangements are currently fragmented, with numerous individual programmes operating in different contexts and locations. Little information is available regarding who is covered by these programmes, what impact these programmes have and how much they cost. This limits the transparency of the social protection sector, reduces the efficiency of programmes and will undermine efforts to create a social protection system. Nonetheless, Cambodia is well-placed to improve this situation through the IDPoor database and the Cambodia Socio-Economic Survey (CSES).

The IDPoor database is a reliable and well-established social registry that should be strengthened in support of a new social protection system. It is used by both by the RGC and development partners to assess eligibility for the majority of social protection programmes; its accuracy is reflected by the progressive beneficiary incidence of programmes such as HEF. It is also a well-known and trusted system, recognised throughout rural Cambodia due to its transparent implementation and grievance procedures at the community level. The willingness of local communities to implement and provide feedback to the system makes it unique and an example to other countries.

The SPPF envisages that the IDPoor database will evolve from a social registry to become the basis for a single registry for the poor and vulnerable which can optimise the efficiency of social protection programmes. There are a variety of steps that need to be taken before this can occur, in terms of the scope, timing and coverage of the database. However, in addressing these issues, the RGC can ensure that the IDPoor is a means of improving not only the targeting of social protection policies but also their design and impact.

The first step in expanding the role of the IDPoor would be to include information on social protection programmes, covering enrolment and benefits. It would thus become a nexus of information for the RGC to implement and monitor its social protection system. In its current form, the IDPoor questionnaire contains a scoring section – the proxy means test – as well as a basic non-scoring section capturing special circumstances causing a reduction in living standards such as illnesses, theft or reduced crop production. This section could be enhanced to cover more dimensions of living standards. However, the balance between the benefit of additional information and burden of fielding a longer questionnaire needs to be weighed carefully.

Box 4.4. **Single vs social registries**

When discussing the information base for social protection systems it is important to clarify between two types of registries often mentioned: social and single registries. These two types of registry differ in their functions, characteristics and feasibility.

Single registries gather information from various types of social protection programmes and can be used as a monitoring tool. They can also be merged with various databases, including programme-specific Management Information System (MIS) databases, as well as government databases on taxation or civil registration. Single registries typically include information on the number and characteristics of beneficiaries across social protection programmes and information on transfers received (amount, frequency, type). Single registries can thus facilitate the application and registration process for individuals and households.

Social registries, also known as unified targeting databases, provide information on households on the basis of which their eligibility for poverty-targeted social programmes can be established. They are thus more limited in their scope than single registries, their primary function being the targeting of social protection beneficiaries.

Social registries play an important role in climate-responsive social protection programmes by informing the authorities which households are likely to be most vulnerable in the event of a climate-related shock. This in turn ensures that emergency assistance can be directed to those most at need, sometimes before the shock has even occurred if early warning systems are in place.

Source: Chirchir and Farooq (2016), "Single Registries and Social Registries: clarifying the terminological confusion", *Pathways' Perspectives*, Issue No. 23.

This dilemma can be resolved in part by linking IDPoor to other databases, such as civil registration or social insurance data. This would allow policy makers to crosscheck information across various sources, thereby facilitating application processes and increasing the accuracy of information.

The IDPoor database needs to be updated more frequently to ensure data quality and accurate targeting. With survey waves carried out, on average, every three years, the system is at risk from errors of exclusion and inclusion, especially given the extensive transitioning in and out of poverty and the high levels of internal migration. Additionally, the SPPF specifically targets vulnerable groups such as pregnant women and children under five, who would need to be accurately registered to become beneficiaries. Increasing the frequency of survey waves will make IDPoor a more reliable source of information on the current poverty status of households.

On-demand registration can mitigate low survey frequency. The incorporation within the IDPoor database of households designated as poor through HEF's post-identification mechanism is a compromise to improve accuracy until an on-demand identification process can be implemented nationwide. The current post-identification mechanism does not match the quality of the IDPoor process due to its simpler and non-participatory procedure. Additionally, the Ministry of Planning (MoP) is currently evaluating various options aimed at allowing greater flexibility in on-demand identification, including electronic data collection through commune councils at district level.

IDPoor's focus on rural areas has restricted access to social programmes; achieving national coverage of the database is an integral part of scaling up social protection itself. With the discrepancy between rural and urban poverty rates decreasing significantly in recent years, the extension of the IDPoor system to urban areas, piloted in 2016, would be an important step towards improving access to social protection for the urban poor. Rolling out the IDPoor database across the entire country will not only improve social protection policies but can also support decentralisation reforms by providing information to local governments to adjust policies to the needs and characteristics of their vulnerable populations.

At the same time as the IDPoor system is transitioning towards a single registry, the CSES could become a high-level monitoring and evaluation tool for social protection. The CSES is nationally representative and conducted annually but its value for social protection planners is so far limited. The survey currently only provides household level data on uptake of broad categories of social protection programmes and the possession of an Equity Card for accessing HEF. Including a more detailed module to capture information on the recipients of social protection would allow for regular, nationally representative stock-taking.

Adding individual and programme-specific data would allow for assessment of targeting mechanisms, uptake rates and adequacy of specific benefits. This would be particularly useful given the breadth of information on individuals and households contained in the CSES, which would allow for detailed analysis of social protection in relation to individual characteristics, such as employment, assets, consumption and education. Over time, the CSES should become an important monitoring and evaluation tool for the social protection system, though it would still need to be complemented by individual programme evaluations.

Processing and delivery mechanisms

Uptake of social protection programmes globally is often hindered by potential beneficiaries not being aware of the benefits for which they might be eligible or lacking information about or access to programmes. Cambodia is particularly prone because it has very few national social protection programmes and the delivery mechanism for even the largest programmes, such as HEF, is fragmented (ILO, 2012). Improving awareness and providing counselling on eligibility could enhance the performance of the social protection system.

Portability or flexible access to social protection transfers is an important delivery issue. Households identified through IDPoor as eligible for certain benefits may not be able to access them outside their locality. This is a particular challenge in Cambodia, given the high levels of internal migration and the lack of national schemes. Alleviating this requires integration of delivery mechanisms, in particular payment mechanisms, as seen in Mexico, Brazil and Colombia (Box 4.5).

A one-stop-shop embedded in government institutions that delivers multiple services (from information dissemination to enrolment and service provision) can realise efficiency gains for providers and enhance programme uptake by simplifying the process for beneficiaries. As such, a single window service facilitates access for poor households by reducing travel and time costs associated with accessing social protection services. It would also contribute to the extension of programme coverage, improve transparency and facilitate information-sharing across government institutions. By fostering horizontal and vertical integration, these services can strengthen sub-national authorities.

A Social Service Delivery Mechanism was piloted by the ILO until 2016 as a means to unify registration and benefit payments. This pilot revealed a need for decentralised case management for social protection programmes that can be performed on a rolling basis.

Box 4.5. **Electronic benefits payment in Mexico, Brazil and Colombia**

New payment mechanisms can multiply the livelihood and empowerment impact of social protection programmes while improving delivery performance, cost-efficiency and value for money. Governments have two options for benefit transfers: the traditional "pull" mechanism, whereby beneficiaries collect their benefits from fixed pay points; or "push" systems, which deliver funds directly to beneficiary bank accounts, smart cards or mobile phones. While most benefit payment systems globally employ "pull" approaches, many countries are piloting or have transitioned to "push" systems.

Mexico's cash transfer programme, Prospera (formerly known as Oportunidades and Progresa at different points in time), established in 1997, employs an electronic payment system to deliver benefits to bank accounts. The system lowers government delivery expenses and private beneficiary costs, while improving delivery reliability. Moreover, the system deepens the programme's developmental impact by promoting and strengthening beneficiary access to financial services. A recent study demonstrates that the payment mechanism changes beneficiary behaviour; they reduce their reliance on informal lending sources and are better able to cope with shocks using their savings

Box 4.5. **Electronic benefits payment in Mexico, Brazil and Colombia** *(cont.)*

rather than suffering a decline in consumption or resorting to often usurious loans (Masino and Niño-Zarazúa, 2014).

Brazil's Bolsa Familia cash transfer programme is another successful example of electronic payment. The broad footprint of Caixa, Brazil's state-run rural development bank, enabled a shift to bank account payments, lowering costs to beneficiaries by 5.8% and deepening beneficiary access to financial services. However, not all countries in Latin America have immediately succeeded in lowering costs using financially inclusive mechanisms. Colombia's shift from cash payments to account-based transfers actually increased the delivery cost from USD 5.20 to USD 6.24 (Bold, Porteous and Rotman, 2012). In the absence of cost-effective banking infrastructure, a dedicated manual cash payment system may provide easier and lower-cost access for beneficiaries. However, it comes with the potential disadvantages of increased fiduciary risks, possible leakages, time-consuming verification processes and the foregone opportunities to provide financial, communications and information services that can enhance livelihood development.

References

Bold, C., D. Porteous and S. Rotman (2012), "Social cash transfers and financial inclusion: Evidence from four countries", *CGAP Focus Notes*, No. 77, Consultative Group to Assist the Poor, Washington, D.C., *cgap.org/sites/default/files/Focus-Note-Social-Cash-Transfers-and-Financial-Inclusion-Evidence-from-Four-Countries-Feb-2012.pdf*.

Chirchir, R. and S. Farooq (2016), "Single Registries and Social Registries: clarifying the terminological confusion", *Pathways' Perspectives*, Issue No. 23, November, Development Pathways, London.

Heckman, J. (2008), "The case for investing in disadvantaged young children", in *Big ideas for children: Investing in our nation's future*, First Focus, Washington, DC, pp. 49-58.

ILO (2017), "Recent trade policy developments and possible implications for Cambodia's garment and footwear sector", *Cambodian Garment and Footwear Sector Bulletin*, Iss. 5, International Labour Organization, Geneva, *ilo.org/asia/publications/WCMS_541288/lang--en/index.htm*.

ILO (2012), *Cambodia: Toward Integrated Employment and Social Protection Policies*, EU/ILO Project on Improving Social Protection and Promoting Employment, International Labour Organization, Geneva, *ilo.org/wcmsp5/groups/public/---europe/---ro-geneva/---ilo-brussels/documents/publication/wcms_196019.pdf*.

Masino, S. and M. Niño-Zarazúa (2014), "Social service delivery and access to financial innovation: The impact of Oportunidades' electronic payment system in Mexico", *UNU-WIDER Working Paper 2014/034*, United Nations University-World Institute for Development Economics Research, Helsinki, *wider.unu.edu/publication/social-service-delivery-and-access-financial-innovation*.

Missoni, E. and G. Solimano (2010), "Towards Universal Health Coverage: the Chilean experience", *World Health Report 2010 Background Paper*, World Health Organization, Geneva, *who.int/healthsystems/topics/financing/healthreport/4Chile.pdf*.

National Bank of Cambodia (2016), "Cambodia Balance of Payments Statistics Bulletin – Series No.54, Fourth Quarter 2016", National Bank of Cambodia, Royal Government of Cambodia, Phnom Penh, *nbc.org.kh/download_files/economic_research/bop_eng/BOP-Bulletin-No-54.pdf*.

NIS and MoP (2011), "Pilot Survey 2010 of 2011 Economic Census of Cambodia", National Institute of Statistics, Ministry of Planning, Royal Government of Cambodia, Phnom Penh, *nada-nis.gov.kh/index.php/catalog/28/related_materials*.

OECD (2017), *OECD.Stat* (database), *stats.oecd.org*, (accessed May 2017).

Tandon, A. et al. (2016), *Indonesia - Health financing system assessment : spend more, right, and better*, World Bank Group, Washington, DC, *documents.worldbank.org/curated/en/453091479269158106/Indonesia-Health-financing-system-assessment-spend-more-right-and-better*.

THL (forthcoming), *The Capacity Assessment for the Coordination and Implementation of Social Assistance Programs in Cambodia*, The National Institute for Health and Welfare [THL], Helsinki.

ORGANISATION FOR ECONOMIC CO-OPERATION AND DEVELOPMENT

The OECD is a unique forum where governments work together to address the economic, social and environmental challenges of globalisation. The OECD is also at the forefront of efforts to understand and to help governments respond to new developments and concerns, such as corporate governance, the information economy and the challenges of an ageing population. The Organisation provides a setting where governments can compare policy experiences, seek answers to common problems, identify good practice and work to co-ordinate domestic and international policies.

The OECD member countries are: Australia, Austria, Belgium, Canada, Chile, the Czech Republic, Denmark, Estonia, Finland, France, Germany, Greece, Hungary, Iceland, Ireland, Israel, Italy, Japan, Korea, Latvia, Luxembourg, Mexico, the Netherlands, New Zealand, Norway, Poland, Portugal, the Slovak Republic, Slovenia, Spain, Sweden, Switzerland, Turkey, the United Kingdom and the United States. The European Union takes part in the work of the OECD.

OECD Publishing disseminates widely the results of the Organisation's statistics gathering and research on economic, social and environmental issues, as well as the conventions, guidelines and standards agreed by its members.

OECD DEVELOPMENT CENTRE

The OECD Development Centre was established in 1962 as an independent platform for knowledge sharing and policy dialogue between OECD member countries and developing economies, allowing these countries to interact on an equal footing. Today, 27 OECD countries and 25 non-OECD countries are members of the Centre. The Centre draws attention to emerging systemic issues likely to have an impact on global development and more specific development challenges faced by today's developing and emerging economies. It uses evidence-based analysis and strategic partnerships to help countries formulate innovative policy solutions to the global challenges of development.

For more information on the Centre and its members, please see *www.oecd.org/dev*.

OECD PUBLISHING, 2, rue André-Pascal, 75775 PARIS CEDEX 16
(41 2017 211 P1) ISBN 978-92-64-28221-6 – 2017

www.ingramcontent.com/pod-product-compliance
Lightning Source LLC
Chambersburg PA
CBHW041324210926
51847CB00003B/41
* 9 7 8 9 2 6 4 2 8 2 2 1 6 *